M.Hyde   01477.571342

TAKE MARY
TO THE
PICTURES

TAKE MARY TO THE PICTURES

A FIGHTER PILOT IN BURMA 1941-1945

By

ALAN 'KIT' KITLEY

Published By:
Coston,
Congleton
Cheshire
CW12 3BH
Tel. 01260 275895

© Copyright 2003
Alan Kitley

The right of Alan Kitley to be identified as the author of
this work has been asserted by him in accordance with the
Copyright, Designs and Patents Act 1988.

All Rights Reserved
No reproduction, copy or transmission of this publication
may be made without written permission.
No paragraph of this publication may be reproduced,
copied or transmitted save with the written permission or in accordance
with the provisions of the Copyright Act 1956 (as amended).
Any person who does any unauthorised act in relation to
this publication may be liable to criminal
prosecution and civil claims for damage.

First published in 2003

ISBN: 0-9546097-0-0

Printed by:
ProPrint
Riverside Cottages
Old Great North Road
Stibbington
Cambs. PE8 6LR

ACKNOWLEDGEMENT

My thanks to Jennie Mackay, Ron Plumpton and Doreen Sturdy for their help and advice in the preparation of the script and material for this book.

DEDICATION

*To my grandchildren:
Matthew, Rachel, Kate, Anthony, Daniel, Amy and Philip who encouraged me to write this book.*

INTRODUCTION

In December 1941 the United Kingdom was under the threat of invasion from a German dominated Europe. The North African campaign was going badly with Rommel aiming to break through Egypt and dominate the Middle East. Thus when the Japanese attacked Pearl Harbour and within weeks overran most of South East Asia there were few fighting units available that could be sent to reinforce the weak defences of Burma. But Burma was important strategically; it was the gateway to India and a Japanese occupied India could have had a profound influence on the future of the war.

In January 1942 I was a pilot member of a newly formed squadron equipped with hurricanes which was ordered to fly from Egypt to Rangoon to provide an air defence of Burma. The Japanese had already started to attack and by the end of March 1942 had gained control of Burma. By that time the remnants of the squadron were back in Calcutta licking their wounds. It was to be a further 3½ years before Burma was reoccupied and Japan surrendered.

The book recounts how, from a fighter pilot's perspective, the air war developed. It describes the wide range and variety of operations that were flown. Also the problems and difficulties faced by the ground support staff and pilots operating within both a hostile man-made and natural environment. The fighting was intense; the casualties high.

Back at home in Britain concern was focussed on the German threat; there was a lack of awareness of what was happening in Burma. Thus the services there came to be known collectively as 'The Forgotten Army'. At Kohima where one of the decisive battles was fought, an epitaph was inscribed on a simple memorial.

> When you go home
> Tell them of us and say
> For their tomorrow
> We gave our today

When I hear those moving words I focus my thoughts on the many pilot friends I flew with and who were killed. The words are a plea to those fortunate to have survived to let them at home know of the significance and extent of their sacrifice. I hope my story helps in fulfilling that plea – 'tell them of us'.

Alan 'Kit' Kitley

CONTENTS

Chapter One	Moosejaw In Mid-winter	1
Chapter Two	Go East Young Man	17
Chapter Three	Air Display For A Sheikh	25
Chapter Four	The Red Road Runway	39
Chapter Five	Dusting The General	51
Chapter Six	Is This What They Call A 'Rest?'	67
Chapter Seven	Punting In Poona	89
Chapter Eight	Looking Back, Looking Forward	109
Maps		117

CHAPTER ONE

MOOSEJAW IN MID-WINTER

Many of my generation will look back to Sunday, 3rd September 1939 and recall the significant influence it had on all our lives. I was living in the suburbs of London, in the village of Hampton Wick, which was on the opposite side of the Thames from Kingston. Being seventeen years of age, the prospect of a war in which I could become involved, was too good to be true; indeed, as with most youngsters of my age, my concern was that the war may be over before I could join up.

My disappointment and annoyance to discover that I could not enter the Services before I was eighteen years old, was not ameliorated by the knowledge that my brother, who in 1938 joined the RAF Volunteer Reserve as a pilot under training, had immediately been called up. He was twenty three years old and the six years difference in our ages meant that throughout most of our teen years, we had tolerated rather than enjoyed each other's company. My widowed mother, who had been born and brought up in London, and whose family had suffered fatalities during the First World War, was naturally concerned for the safety of her elder son. At the same time, she was thankful that her younger son was too young to join the Services, and like many in those days thought that the war would be over within a few months. As it was, the air raid sirens that sounded shortly after Mr Neville Chamberlain's declaration of war, proved to be a false alarm and after the initial excitement the country settled down to the anticlimax of experiencing the war that never seemed to come; the so called phoney war, - pamphlets but not bombs; threats but no action. But to most mums, and mine in particular, this lack of action was seized on gratefully; little Alan was safe!

During this phoney war period which lasted roughly to the Spring of 1940, (Poland was the only country where phoney war had not applied), the daily press maintained a momentum of interest by printing maps for households to pin to their walls, showing the sizes and dispositions of all the services likely to become involved. There were different pins for tanks, ships, aeroplanes, and colours denoted who would be on our side, on Germany's side, and those so-called neutral countries who were sitting on the sidelines. The disposition of the pins was altered daily according to new press intelligence information. What we did not realise at the time was that the size of the various allied forces was a false indication of strength; most of the planes, tanks and ships were obsolete and would prove ineffective when the real war started.

In late 1939, and early 1940, I was working as a draughtsman in the estimating department of a construction company in Fleet Street, London. My salary was seventeen shillings and six pence per week and out of this I paid ten shillings for a Southern Railway season ticket, two shillings and six pence towards my keep, and five shillings for myself. The company, being (on reflection) farsighted, decided to evacuate their London office to the site of their works at Rickmansworth, Hertfordshire. As the journey from Hampton Wick to Rickmansworth involved three trains taking two hours, I stayed with an aunt and uncle who lived in Harrow, a short journey from Rickmansworth.

I soon got fed up with this arrangement and decided that until I could join the RAF at eighteen years of age, I would get a job in my local area. I succeeded. I got a job in Bentalls store in Kingston-on-Thames as a salesman in the Sports Department at two pounds per week. I was thrilled; double the pay and no travelling expenses! My mother and her brothers and sisters were appalled. Youths who had gained a matriculation certificate were destined to follow a career in a profession, and in their book, becoming a salesman in Bentalls was not the start of a career with a promising future. A family conference was called. The manager of the company employing me attended; he said that I had an excellent future with the company and my action had disappointed him.

The men in the family, who in the main followed so-called respectable careers, were against me. There was one exception; my mother's younger brother supported me, but as he had recently returned from Australia having led a strike in the Sydney docks and was showing socialist tendencies, his opinions did not, in the eyes of his three sisters and four brothers, carry any weight. He was later criticised for taking me off to a pub and buying me a beer; in the eyes of the others this showed how suspect his opinions were.

I was forced to leave Bentalls and to return to the construction company and living at Harrow. I was given a five shillings a week raise. But frankly I was fed up with all that had happened and had I had a more independent confidence building upbringing, plus the language to go with it, I might have told them all to 'Sod off!' As it was, my love and respect for my mother led me to go along with the decision. However, what made a real impact on me was that the manager of my employing company had indicated, at the family conference, that my job was on the Government's reserved occupation list and that I would not be able to join the Forces when I was eighteen years old. It was this that made me determined to join the RAF as soon as possible and before I was eighteen, and if I could, become a pilot.

It was now the Spring of 1940 and the German army was on the move. They outflanked a demoralised and incompetent French army and headed for the French ports; Dunkirk was imminent. I was determined to join up and if necessary lie about my age. I phoned my company and explained that I was sick. I left my aunt's in the mornings and returned in the evenings. I spent three days going around the recruitment centres in the London area. I got nowhere; at every centre I was asked for my birth certificate; if I showed it I was told to come back when I was eighteen, if I said I did not have one I was told to go and get one. My breakthrough occurred at Willesden. I was going through the recruitment interview when a corporal interrupted and told the interviewing sergeant that he was wanted on the phone. The corporal took over and asked me where he had got to; I explained that the sergeant had confirmed from my birth certificate that I was eighteen. He accepted this and for the next thirty years was to follow an RAF career based on my birthday being on 15th June 1922 and not 15th July 1922; only a difference of four weeks but very significant in the influence this would have on my future.

The interviewing corporal then explained that I had two choices. I could be enrolled as a potential pilot and return to civilian life until I was called up to undergo aptitude and medical tests for acceptance as a pilot under training. The alternative was to enrol immediately into the RAF as an aircraft hand general duties (ACH/GD) and wait until I was called forward for pilot training tests. Realising the problems that I would meet if I took the former option and returned home, I readily accepted the second.

Events then took over. I joined a group of new recruits and after a brief medical examination, which as I recall centred on ensuring that when I coughed exciting things happened in the area of my private parts, we were inoculated, vaccinated and sworn on the Bible, allegiance to the Crown. It then became very apparent that we were now in the RAF; words such as 'please,' 'thank you' 'if you would not mind' and so on had now given place to 'do this,' 'go there,' 'be quiet' etc. Marshalled into a coach, we then set off on a three hour journey to RAF Cardington where we were to undergo initial training.

I cannot recall in detail our reception at Cardington; I phoned my mother with the news (which caused her distress). I do remember clearly being bedded down in a bell tent with some twenty recruits, mainly conscripts and generally much older than myself. It was after lights out and one of the group suggested that we get to know each other by calling out who we were and what we were going to do in the RAF. This was agreed and it soon became apparent that we were a very mixed bunch with trades such as cooks, clerks, police, armourers, riggers etc. etc. I was the last to call out my name and proposed trade, and remember the acute embarrassment when I proclaimed that I hoped to become a pilot. This triggered off responses such as 'Christ, - we've got a bloody Air Marshall with us,' 'He's a little four letter word,' 'Must be a public school twit' and so on. I think I started to cry, but not noticeably, and decided there and then that I had now joined a man's world and must quickly get with it and make sure I could give as well as I got.

After a week at Cardington we were sent to Blackpool for two weeks initial training and billeted in boarding houses. Three aspects of my training remain vivid in my mind. Firstly, we drilled every day on the promenade with drill sergeants entertaining the crowds of holidaymakers with ribald comments at our expense. Secondly, lectures which centred on the terrible consequences of getting a venereal disease and advocating a life of celibacy. Thirdly, salt and brass buttons are not good bedfellows and cleaning buttons four times a day became a must if you were to avoid the wrath of the NCOs.

After Blackpool the recruits were sent throughout the country to the various trade-training establishments. I became a problem for the administration. I must have been one of the first volunteers to join up while awaiting the call for pilot acceptance and training. I remember a sergeant saying to the officer 'better send him back to Cardington.' This they did.

Back at Cardington I was put in a ground gunner section, and trained in rifle and hand grenade activities. When we were not training we were on duty protecting the two enormous airship hangers from God knows what? It sounded important, but being in a slit trench in the middle of the night in pouring rain with no apparent threat, soon brought us down to earth. After some four weeks I was sent for by the Officer in Charge and told I was being confirmed in the trade of ground gunner and being promoted to the rank of corporal. I told the officer that I was awaiting the call for aircrew selection, and did not want to be a corporal ground gunner. He replied he knew nothing about that and I would do as I was told, and that if my attitude did not change he would withdraw the promotion to corporal. I felt double-crossed, lonely and without a friend, apart from another ground gunner whom I discovered had joined up under the same conditions as myself. We asked for an interview with a more senior officer and were told that it would be a few days before it could be arranged and that it wouldn't do any good anyway. It was becoming apparent that we would be unlikely to get a sympathetic hearing if indeed we got a hearing at all. We were both determined to take over control of our fate if we could, and gaining strength from each other, decided to abscond and go to the Air Ministry in London. We climbed through the camp perimeter fence in the middle of the night and walked the five miles to Bedford railway station looking out for the military police; for during the war, all servicemen had to carry an authority to be absent from their Unit;

and this for obvious reasons we did not have. We caught a very early train to London via Retford. I remember the 'via' very clearly because it meant we could be further exposed to approaches by the police while waiting at that station. On arrival in London we presented ourselves at Adastral House in Kingsway, - two bedraggled airmen with no passes and trying to explain to a doorman why we were there. The RAF police were sent for and had it not been for a police sergeant who was prepared to listen to our story, we would have been immediately returned to Cardington under arrest. As it was we were eventually interviewed by an officer who gave us a good hearing, a thorough dressing down, phoned and informed Cardington that we would be returning that day and suggested Cardington should charge us on arrival with absence without leave. But, and here was the good news, he confirmed that we would be called forward for aircrew selection in the near future; he added, 'Well done,' and wished us both the best of luck. At Cardington we were charged, put in the guardroom overnight and given a summary sentence of confinement to camp with extra drill and duties of a somewhat unpleasant nature. Within two weeks we were both called forward for aircrew selection.

The aircrew selection progress took place over two days and included, in addition to various aptitude and other tests, a very thorough medical examination. We were told beforehand that the outcome would be either rejection, or acceptance for training as either a pilot, navigator, wireless operator or air gunner. Here now was another hurdle to overcome. I would have accepted any one of the categories of aircrew available in preference to rejection, but my heart was set on becoming a pilot. During the two day selection process I was continually measuring myself against the other applicants. Rumours ran rife; the 'know all' applicants were saying that only one in ten was selected as pilots and that four out of ten were rejected as potential aircrew. The more rumours I heard, the more my morale suffered, and it was with genuine surprise and unbounded delight that I heard that I had been accepted as a pilot under training. I had made it thus far but faced up to the realisation that novice hurdlers had a long way to go before they could qualify for Aintree.

Within a short space of time orders came through for me to report to an initial training wing (ITW) at Torquay. I left Cardington wearing the white flash on my cap, the insignia for pilots under training, promoted to a Leading Aircraftman (LAC) and with my pay increased from two shillings and six pence to seven shillings and six pence per day. The training was to involve eight weeks in Torquay studying all the subjects relevant to training for a pilot, in addition to extensive physical training programmes. I enjoyed that eight weeks. The accommodation was in one of the many hotels that the RAF had taken over, - spartan but comfortable - overlooking Torbay. The studies were intensive and the hurdle was to ensure that you passed the examinations; if you did not then you were out. It was September/October 1940, the weather was glorious and it took a German Messerschmidt, which one day dived and shot at random at Torquay and its environs, to remind us that there was a real war going on. I suffered, as did the others, the tension of hearing the exam results and was relieved then that the hurdle was behind me. These results were critical; there were no resits, no re-coursing; you either passed or failed and if you failed then you lost your white flash and suffered your pay going back to two shillings and six pence per day - and no more hopes of becoming a pilot.

Following Torquay, some five of us were posted to an elementary flying school (EFTS) at Marshalls of Cambridge. Marshalls was a civilian flying school but had been reinforced with RAF instructors and mechanics to cope with the increased demand for flying training. I was billeted with a lady whose husband was in the Army having been evacuated from Dunkirk. She had been forced to accept one RAF trainee in her home and as I recall was obsessed with the belief that the virginity of her fifteen year old daughter was under threat. Little did she know that I wouldn't have known what to do anyway. I also did not think much of her daughter. However she was very kind and treated me quite well, - I mean the mother!

But the real test, the steeplechase fences, now faced us. Regardless of our studies and exams, medical and physical fitness, white flashes and extra pay, the criteria for success now depended on the ability to learn to successfully pilot an aeroplane; to take up an aeroplane and land it on your own. The conditions laid down were stringent. The RAF could not invest costly resources in developing unsuitable talent, and so it was made clear to each trainee that they had to be able to fly solo within a maximum of eight hours instruction in the air. If after eight hours this had not been achieved then the trainee would be given a 'check out' flight with the chief flying instructor; then after discussion with the trainee's instructor he would decide either to suspend the trainee from flying or allow a further two hours instruction. If after this the trainee was still not fit to be authorised to fly solo, automatic suspension followed. I do not know of the failure rate statistics but believe it was in the order of 30%.

      I recall two incidents during my initial flying training on Tiger Moths. The first was getting completely lost on my second solo flight. From above, the British landscape can present a panoramic complexity of roads, railways, villages etc. and I panicked, flying in all directions hoping to suddenly find my airfield. I decided to find a railway line and follow it to a station where I could read the name on the platform; a somewhat hazardous operation for an experienced pilot, but foolhardy for one on his second solo flight. I circled a railway station three or four times at low level, but only succeeded in scaring the living daylights out of the waiting passengers. I was now running out of fuel and force landed in a school playing field, fortunately without damaging the aeroplane. I reported to the police and while waiting enjoyed the admiration of the children who had decided that I was a war ace. The school field was too small to allow the aircraft to take off and it had to be transported by road back to Cambridge. On the way back, my instructor, who had come out in the hope that he could fly the Tiger Moth back to Cambridge, warned me that I would receive a hot reception on arrival. Thus I had to await the possibility or indeed the likelihood, that I would be suspended. The interview with the chief flying instructor made its mark on me but he decided that I could continue training.

      The other incident was landing one day and noticing some holes in the fabric of the Tiger Moth. There had been a German aircraft in the area and bursts of firing had been heard from the ground. It was assumed that I had been attacked as an opportunity target but not realised it. My instructor suggested I was concentrating hard on not getting lost again! When the course was completed I had forty two hours in my logbook including twenty two hours solo. I look back and wonder how we managed to master the flying. Winter in an open cockpit wearing thick fur lined jackets, trousers and flying boots along with silk and woollen gloves under heavy leather gauntlets, made the sensitivity of touch needed to control a Tiger Moth with hands and feet, almost impossible.

Following this initial flying training, trainees were selected to go on to a service flying training school (SFTS) to fly more advanced aircraft and of a type more likely to equip them for the operational flying for which they had been selected ie. fighters, bombers etc. I was overjoyed on being told that I had been recommended for a fighter aircraft role and would be going for training on Harvards, a powerful single engined aircraft. When I asked my instructor on leaving why I had been selected for the prestigious role of fighter pilot, he replied that only a 'round the bend' trainee would successfully land a Tiger Moth in a school playing field; would get shot at by a German fighter aircraft without realising it; would try to read the name of a railway station without knowing that all place names and signposts throughout the country had been removed in case of invasion; and that fighter pilots were in his opinion 'round the bend'. My friend, who had been with me since we absconded from Cardington, was earmarked for bomber operations and sent for training on the twin engined Oxford aircraft. We never met again. He was subsequently killed flying a Wellington bomber over Germany.

Five of us arrived at RAF Tern Hill, Shropshire, for flying training on Harvards, only to find that the school was moving to Canada and in particular to Moosejaw, Saskatchewan. To widen our experience of service life, we spent a week or so working in the kitchens and toilets of the Officers' Mess before embarking at Liverpool for Halifax, Nova Scotia. We were on a passenger ship, which had been converted into a troopship, and the conditions were appalling. I was on G deck. well below the waterline, where there were some twenty tables. Each table was home for some twenty men who sat, ate, slept (in hammocks) and, if they couldn't get to the head of the latrines queue in time, were seasick. Each deck was allowed to exercise in turn on the promenade deck. As it was now mid-winter with short daylight hours the ration for each deck was one hour per day. Although being let out into fresh air sounded attractive, the promenade deck on a ship in the North Atlantic in mid-winter had limited appeal.

On arrival at Halifax our conditions changed completely. The journey to Moosejaw took three days and we went by Canadian Pacific Railway with all the facilities and comforts of fare paying passengers; first class food (no rationing), dining cars, sleeping cars; and at every step we were welcomed by the local population as though we were war heroes. At certain stops we were allowed to get off the train for up to two hours and accept the hospitality of residents.

Moosejaw turned out to be a very friendly, homely and pleasant town, completely isolated from the war and its restrictions. We were made most welcome. I remember so clearly the Exchange Café near the railway station where a waitress, Ruth, used to give me pumpkin pie with a double helping of thick cream which, after we got to know each other, never appeared on the bill. But our stay at Moosejaw was only some eight weeks and apart from Ruth, the only features I now recall were an ice hockey stadium, a radio station, a cinema, difficulty in getting booze, and very friendly relations with the townsfolk.

Learning to fly Harvard aircraft in Moosejaw in mid-winter was an experience not to be repeated. The temperature at times went as low as 60 degrees Fahrenheit below freezing point, -92 degrees of frost! Every morning a force of snowploughs was out on the airfield levelling and crushing the overnight snow. Fortunately the single engined monoplane Harvard had an enclosed cockpit and a very effective heating system, and if it wasn't snowing the weather was normally clear and a dry atmosphere tempered the effect of the intense cold. However for us, still learning to fly, the crushed snow formed an icy surface which, coupled with rough handling of the rudder controls, could cause the Harvard to ground loop on landing; this in turn could result in a collapsed undercarriage and a severe bollocking from a senior flying instructor. Whereas air navigation in

England was made complex by a concentration of roads, railways etc. in Saskatchewan all you could see from the air was a white panorama speckled by the odd black blodge of small towns; however I did manage not to get lost again. But I do believe that learning to fly in such adverse conditions equipped the trainees with landing and navigation skills they might not have attained in more idealistic circumstances. After some fifty hours flying on Harvards, coupled with forty two hours on Tiger Moths, I was awarded my 'wings' and promoted to sergeant.

The author 'Kit' Kitley
I've Got My Wings

It was now early March 1941. The training of aircrews in Canada under the Empire Air Training Scheme, was by now producing trained pilots and navigators which were urgently needed for the build up of our air forces in the UK. Our passage back to Halifax was expedited, but on arrival we learnt that the shipping losses in the North Atlantic had seriously reduced the availability of passages to the UK. The RCAF had thus been forced to turn a newly built airfield at Debert into a holding transit camp for those awaiting passage to the UK. Unfortunately, although the runways and hangers had been constructed the accommodation blocks were still under construction, and for the two - three weeks we waited at Debert we lived in a large aircraft hangar in which were some one hundred double tiered beds. Tempers were frayed; no arrangements had been made for RAF personnel to be paid; to get to the field kitchen and temporary toilet facilities meant walking on narrow wooden planks to avoid the deep mud resulting from the Spring thaw. During the war I learnt the words of many songs which embryo poets had produced and I remember very few. However I will always recall the last verse of a rendering dedicated to Debert, which went as follows:

> This camp is situated in the middle of a bog
> When you walk you sink in shit up to your knees
> Oh this bloody awful station
> Is the arsehole of creation
> And we'll all be pleased when we're across the seas.

Eventually, some fifteen of us were given passage to the UK aboard a Royal Navy armed merchant vessel. Such ships had been modified from passenger to fighting ships by the mounting of half a dozen six-inch guns and depth charge launching equipment. They tended to be crewed by reservists and those recalled to service after retirement. Many will recall that these ships and their brave crews suffered severe casualties in their determination to defend the North Atlantic convoys from attacks by U-boat and surface battleships. Also this period, winter 1940/41 saw a peak build up of such casualties. The sinking of the armed merchant ship HMS Rawalpindi in defending a convoy by attacking on its own a pocket battleship, exemplifies this bravery.

When we boarded our ship at Halifax we were addressed by the captain who made us welcome by making it clear that he did not want passengers on board his fighting ship; that he had protested to no avail to higher authority; that we would be housed in the ship's gymnasium which would have to be available at certain hours for recreation activities for the crew; that although we were sergeants we could not use the Petty Officers' Mess; and that he hoped he would not see any of us again before disembarking in the UK.

This somewhat unenthusiastic welcome permeated the ship's crew whose attitude was a reflection of the hostility shown by their captain. We were then addressed by the Master of Arms who explained that two Hotchkiss guns would be mounted on either side of the ship, and that we were to arrange a manning schedule to ensure that throughout each 24-hour day there were two of us manning each gun. The Hotchkiss gun was a semi-obsolete machine gun and what use it could be in a storm, at night, in the North Atlantic against a surface-raider made us realise that the true purpose of the operation was triggered by the vindictiveness of the captain.

However, we did as we were told (could we do otherwise?) but on the third day out and at 3.00am in a storm, with ice building up on the gun, I collapsed and was taken to the sick bay where a most charming, albeit somewhat alcoholic, bearded Lieutenant Commander Doctor declared that I had double pneumonia. (Trust me to go for a double!). While in the sick bay I was given every consideration and medical help. A medical orderly tended me day and night, and the doctor, who was somewhat of a naval historian, entertained me by firing a small cannon which shot a ball bearing with great force that ricocheted around the sick bay.

When the convoy arrived off Iceland, I was still pretty sick and the medical officer recommended that I be sent to hospital at Reykjavik. I was wrapped and strapped into a cane type structure and hoisted by crane over the ship's side onto a small Icelandic tugboat. I was put, strapped up, into the galley which was cramped, hot and airless; and whenever one of the crew of two looked in I tried to indicate that I needed to be unstrapped but, unable to gesticulate or converse, I remained like that until we arrived at Reykjavik where a nurse spent some time massaging my cramped body before putting me into an ambulance.

I was on the seriously ill register for a week or so before moving into a general ward and some two weeks later declared fully fit. I now awaited instructions on how to get to England. Nobody knew and, in a sense, nobody cared, - I was not their responsibility. I went into Reykjavik and reported to the Royal Naval authorities.

They were very co-operative and arranged for me to embark on one of two destroyers due to escort a convoy to Scotland.

When we sailed out of Reykjavik on 22nd May 1941 we witnessed a sight I will never forget. The mighty HMS Hood and the newly commissioned battleship, HMS Prince of Wales, along with escorting cruisers and destroyers were setting sail to intercept and sink the Bismarck. I had a bit of luck in that a decision had been made to detach the other escorting destroyer to join the Hood's escort and leave only the one destroyer, mine, to escort the convoy of some thirty ships to the Clyde. Imagine the disbelief and bewilderment when we learnt the next day that the Bismarck had sunk the Hood, (only three of the 1,500 ships complement surviving) and severely damaged the Prince of Wales; some of the escorting ships had been sunk and I believe that the destroyer which was detached from my convoy was one of those; hence my bit of luck. To finish this horror story the Bismarck was finally sunk on 27th May, having been struck by torpedo carrying Swordfish aircraft from HMS Victorious, followed by gunfire from two cruisers. I look back on that return from Canada and reflect on the losses incurred by the ships in the convoy; witnessing a tanker blowing up in the middle of the night from U-boat torpedoes and wondering whether we would be next, can create a degree of stress that would make an army of sociology counsellors realise the limitations of their ability and experience.

On arrival at Strathclyde I contacted the RAF Movements Office and became officially recognised and accepted back into the RAF. I was given leave and arrived at my mother's at Hampton Wick proudly sporting my wings and sergeant stripes. I well remember that leave; I met with my three aunts and four uncles and many cousins who lived in the London area; also many of my old school chums. My mother and I went to Dorset to stay for a few days with an aunt on my father's side; a wonderful old lady who was in her seventies. Whenever I appeared in the streets of Bridport I was adulated and regarded, with my wings, as a war hero! There were however embarrassing situations such as when my aunt and mother had me collected by taxi from a public house (my mother and aunt lived in a world where nice people did not go to a pub), where the locals had spent the evening buying me pints of cider which they assured me had little alcoholic content. I soon learnt that naivety was not for one having to grow up quickly. Fortunately, over exposure to cider did not lead me to becoming TT.

The short period that I had with my mother in London brought me face to face with the effects of the war; with the hazards and deprivations being suffered by the civilian population. I learnt with embarrassment that the one egg I was given for my first breakfast was my mother's ration for one month. The gas works and railway line behind our house was bombed during my stay and bullet marks on the house told their own story.

Following my leave I was sent to a holding transit unit in Bournemouth, which was in a very comfortable hotel, and then posted, along with five others, to a fighter operational training unit (FOTU) at RAF Usworth. (Now the site of the Japanese Nissan car factory!). I had not flown for three months and with only ninety six flying hours in my logbook I faced with trepidation my first trip in a Hawker Hurricane. Further, the Hurricane being a single seat aircraft, one did not have the comfort of being able to fly it initially with an instructor. After being given three hours flying in a Miles Majester I was authorised to take my first flight in a Hurricane. I can only equate this experience with that of one, who having driven a saloon car, is then sent off in a formula one racing car.

The problem facing an inexperienced pilot in flying the high speed Hurricane for the first time, was the combination of coping with a rapid build up of speed and with having to change hands on the control column to operate the undercarriage lever. If during this critical take off manoeuvre you looked down to find the undercarriage lever, there was the danger of pressing the control column forward with disastrous results. This was thought to be the reason why one of our five was killed on take-off shortly after our course started.

We were given some twenty hours flying on Hurricanes during which time we had to learn formation flying, air fighting manoeuvres and tactics, low flying, live firing on static and moving targets; all this while trying to develop the ability to fly and control the Hurricane, and incidentally avoid the concentrated barrage balloon defences over Newcastle Upon Tyne some three miles away. There were more casualties. One of our now four trainees was practising dummy attacks on a Manchester bomber operating from a bomber OTU. He flew into the Manchester killing himself and the crew of four. I witnessed this crash while waiting my turn to follow him into the attack. The three of us left were asked to be pallbearers at the funeral of the pilot of the Manchester, in Sunderland. He was twenty years old, an only son, and sitting in the parlour of his house with his father, mother and younger sister after the funeral was a most distressing and sombre experience. These fatalities at Usworth were my first introduction to the realities of death and the implications of the sort of 'World at War' I was becoming involved in. It was also for me the start of the hardening process of having to accept death as an every day event. But with the naive optimism of youth such deaths were for others, not for me.

After some three weeks at Usworth I received orders to join No 136 Fighter Squadron at Kirton-in-Lindsey, Lincolnshire. My reactions and emotions were mixed; thrilled that I was now regarded as a qualified operational fighter pilot; concerned as to whether my flying ability would see me through. My thoughts dwelt on my flying experiences to date: the pressures of taking and passing the many ground and flying examinations and tests; the many worrying experiences that trainee pilots face in the air; relief at making after every sortie a safe landing; the satisfaction of gaining my wings, regrets for those who had failed to reach the required standard; and sympathy for those who had suffered injury or been killed in training. But, overall was the knowledge that I had made it. However, little did I realise that, as with all newly trained pilots, I was ill-equipped to cope with the many known and unknown hazards that would be facing me in the forthcoming flying war years. Finally I was just sensitive enough to feel regret that I had brought many worries to my mother, even though she was by now outwardly showing her pride in having a fighter pilot as a son.

CHAPTER TWO

GO EAST YOUNG MAN

I arrived at Kirton-in-Lindsey in mid August 1941, excited that I was joining a squadron but conscious that I would be the 'rookie' or 'sprog' pilot of the squadron; as such I would have to fly hard and well to become accepted. The anticlimax of being told at the guardroom that they had never heard of 136 Squadron was hard to bear. The written orders I carried clearly stated that I was to join 136 Squadron at Kirton; these made no impression on the guardroom. The station warrant officer took me across to the station headquarters and came out of the adjutant's office mumbling that nobody had bothered to tell him that a squadron was being formed on the station. The doubt he still retained was dispelled the next day when sixteen Hurricanes from Ferry Command landed.

So I found that, rather than being concerned that I would be the 'sprog' pilot in a body of experienced pilots, I was the first pilot to arrive on the squadron, followed on the same day by the squadron commander. As it turned out, within some two weeks approximately twenty five pilots had arrived, with all but two, the squadron and flight commanders, having come direct from training. I am avoiding naming the persons involved in my story, but with the exception of the Squadron Commander, Squadron Leader T A F Elsdon. He was an experienced Battle of Britain pilot who had eventually been shot down and suffered severe damage to one of his legs. He had bullied the medical officers to pass him fit for flying and for guts and leadership I know of no finer man. Indeed he was to have a significant influence on forming my character and I will always be grateful to him.

The squadron commander had received orders that the squadron was to be operational by the end of September. He and the flight commander, had the formidable task of welding a group of 'sprog' pilots into a cohesive and efficient fighting unit. Our only asset was enthusiasm; we studied, trained and flew hard. Accidents occurred but fortunately only one fatality. The fatality involved one of the pilots losing sight of his section leader while forming up for a squadron formation flight. I was in the formation and flying next to the pilot concerned so had a close up view of the accident. The pilot flew under and slightly ahead of his leader; he then climbed and the leader's propeller chopped his Hurricane in two behind the cockpit. I can still recall the look of horror on his face as the wing and cockpit he was left in tipped forward and dived into the ground. But there were less tragic incidents. I recall on one occasion landing and finding the airfield full of parked Hampden bombers; I taxied around looking for the squadron parking area until the realisation came to me that instead of Kirton, I had landed at Scampton, a bomber base. I looked to see if the ground was clear, opened the throttle and flew off landing at Kirton a few minutes later. But I didn't get away with it; the subsequent interview with the squadron commander was memorable. In addition to the pilots there were also some 150 ground personnel - fitters, riggers, armourers, wireless mechanics and many other specialised tradesmen needed to support flying operations. With the exception of a few SNCOs these were also straight from training. So with the help of the engineer officer, the squadron commander had to develop an effective servicing organisation; and in getting everyone, pilots and ground personnel, working together, following the principles of interdependency, he demonstrated effective powers of leadership, management and command.

At the end of September, after some six weeks, the squadron was deemed by Group Headquarters to be fit for fighter operational duties. We were brought on to defensive readiness and also given a role of defending North Sea convoys from air attacks. This was a dangerous activity; not so much because of enemy aircraft, but because the Royal Navy escort ships didn't trust any aircraft that came within range and could not clearly identify itself. The Navy philosophy seemed to be, - if in doubt shoot it!

It was now well into October and the squadron was ordered to prepare for re-deployment. Rumours abounded; we were going south to reinforce the fighter defences in southern England; going to Northern Ireland to intercept the German Condor long range bombers which were attacking our convoys in the Atlantic; being sent with Nos. 17 and 135 Squadrons, to form a fighter wing with the Russians in the Caucasus; or taking our Hurricanes on board the aircraft-carrier HMS Ark Royal in the Mediterranean and flying them off to reinforce Malta which was then under siege.

There was credibility in all these rumours, but they were based on the war situation as it was and not as it was to become by the end of the year. In preparation for the likely reinforcement of Malta, we studied the problem of operating from an aircraft-carrier and practised flying the Hurricanes from short take off runs with two long range fuel tanks fitted under the wings; these were to extend the operating range of the Hurricane so that we could fly off the carrier when it was within approximately 700 miles of Malta. This plan foundered when the Ark Royal was sunk on 13th November and no other suitable aircraft carrier was available.

Reinforcing the Russians in the Caucasus was the next priority and in mid November the pilots and ground crews of 136 and the other two squadrons embarked on the Clyde for, as we thought, the Middle East, where we would pick up our Hurricanes. But while at sea the war situation changed daily. Losses of naval ships in the Mediterranean restricted supplies getting through to reinforce the 8th Army (Desert Rats), which was already extended in North Africa and facing a counter attack by Rommel; this was to result in a 600 mile retreat to Cairo. Reinforcing the Caucasus became a dead duck. Finally, the entry of Japan into the war on 8th December resulted in a complete review of the worldwide war strategy and one which was to see some of us with Hurricanes in Rangoon by the end of January 1942. But much water was to go under the bridge before this outcome. The situation was now, to say the least, confusing and the outline of events that follow is substantially correct although the detail may suffer from memory lapse!

The convoy, with our personnel and some crated Hurricanes which had left the Clyde in November, arrived off Freetown, Sierra Leone, a few days before Christmas 1941. In those days West Africa had the reputation of being the 'white man's grave'. In the eerie, dank heat mist over Freetown one could imagine the cholera, yellow fever, malaria germs etc. having a field day. The journey from the Clyde had been boring, but the accommodation on board if somewhat cramped was comfortable. Before leaving England, I, along with seven other sergeants had been commissioned as pilot officers, and officer accommodation even in wartime, was markedly different from the conditions I had experienced in the troopship to Canada. As an aside I should briefly recount the purchasing of my officer's uniform. My mother had taken me to Gieves in New Regent Street and much to my embarrassment and to the amusement of the tailors, supervised the whole operation as she had done when getting my school uniform!

After signals from and to the Air Ministry and conferences with officials, it was decided that some of the pilots of 136 Squadron would proceed by coastal vessel to Takoradi, pick up Hurricanes there, fly them to Cairo and thence on to Rangoon - a journey of some 13,000 miles. In the meantime the ground crews and remaining pilots would carry on in the convoy around the Cape and hopefully eventually arrive in Singapore, or Rangoon, or India, or dispersed among the three, depending on evolving events.

So, on Christmas Day, we were taken by tender to a rather scruffy looking 4,000 ton ship, which was to take three - four days to get to Takoradi. Our Christmas celebrations lasted those three - four days and significantly helped to develop my ability to both drink and hold my liquor!

At Takoradi, the Hurricanes we were expecting to fly to the Middle East had already left, and had been flown by ferry pilots to reinforce the Middle East Air Force. It became apparent that all military aircraft being assembled at Takoradi were being taken under the control of the Air Commander in Chief, Middle East, regardless of Air Ministry and Government orders. However we did not have to spend undue time in Takoradi; within a day or so we were given passenger tickets and flown to Cairo by Pan American Airlines. In those days, passenger airlines had high standards of passenger comfort. Accommodation and food in the air and on the ground was first class and we enjoyed the trip, stopping at places across Africa such as Kano, Maiduguri, En Genina, El Fasher, Khartoum and up the Nile Valley to Cairo.

On our arrival in Cairo we found Egypt and the Middle East in turmoil. In October/November the 8th Army had successfully relieved Tobruk and pushed Rommel back through Cyrenaica; they were now some 600 miles from Cairo. However due to significant further naval losses in the Mediterranean, our supply ships had been unable to get through to deliver essential petrol, ammunition and the many other resources needed if the 8th Army was to advance further, or at worst hold its position. In the meantime Rommel had received reinforcements and supplies and had started a counter attack with the likelihood of advancing, in a matter of days, back through Cyrenaica to the Egyptian border. Such an advance would threaten the security of the whole of the Middle East and give Germany access to the oilfields of Persia (now Iran). Understandable then, that the Middle East Air Commander was determined to keep our Hurricanes and pilots, to strengthen his air force in what was likely to be a fight for Egypt and the Middle East. The fact that there was a need to reinforce our forces which were taking a pounding in Singapore, Malaya and Burma, was at that time not his problem. Signals flashed back and forth between Cairo and London. While this was going on we spent approximately one-two weeks in a comfortable hotel in Cairo suffering the frustration of not having sufficient money to enjoy to the full the doubtful pleasures of Egyptian nightlife.

However, eventually the Middle East Command was ordered by the Air Ministry to arrange for some thirty six Hurricanes and their pilots to proceed to the Far East as soon as possible, and the first twelve were to be sent immediately. I was included in the first flight of six which was to be led by our squadron commander, with our flight commander leading the second flight of six leaving two days later. Our orders were to get to Rangoon and to get there as soon as possible ready for immediate war operations.

So one early morning in mid January 1942, six of us left our hotel in Cairo in the back of a three ton truck to Kilo 8 airfield some twenty miles from Cairo. It was an uncomfortable, bumpy, dusty ride but the excitement that we were at last on our way kept the adrenaline flowing. At Kilo 8 we each signed for our aircraft and parachute and prepared to take off to air test the aircraft before setting off to Rangoon. A very co-operative airman fitter accompanied me on the pre-flight checks of the aircraft, helped strap me into the cockpit and wished me luck. It was now that I realised that life had become serious. I had some 250 flying hours in my logbook, had not flown since early November, had limited experience of flying a Hurricane and had not experienced aerial combat of any sort. But at that moment my concern was would I be able to take off satisfactorily, carry out the air test drills and manoeuvres, and in particular land the aircraft safely. In the event all went well; I taxied onto the airfield, looked to make sure all was clear for take off (radios had not been fitted) and set off. I landed back thirty minutes later and was able to confirm that the aircraft was fully serviceable and sign to that effect in the aircraft log book (F 700). As for the landing, they say that any landing you can walk away from must be OK. So I was not too concerned when the squadron commander asked me to try not to emulate a kangaroo on my future landings.

We had considered the implications of the trip to Rangoon. The journey envisaged landing at the following airfields: Lydda (Palestine), Habbaniya (Iraq) Bahrain and Sharjah (Persian Gulf), Jiwani, Karachi, Lahore, Delhi, Allahabad and Calcutta (India), Toungoo and Rangoon (Burma). The distance was some 5,500 miles and each stage was between 5 - 600 miles.

Long-range petrol tanks had been fitted to the Hurricanes and we would have to remain aware all the time of the complications of the fuel system and its operation; failure to transfer from reserve, main and long range tanks at the right time could result in engine stoppage. Our concentration and alertness could be weakened by having to fly in stages of up to four hours at heights of between 5,000 and 10,000 feet, where the heat from the desert below and the sun could produce drowsiness similar to that experienced by car drivers on a long journey. We had little knowledge of the likely weather we would meet, apart from knowing that the monsoon period would not have started in India. In the event the weather was placid, but the heat haze over the whole route severely restricted visibility and identification of ground features. Our radios would not be fitted until we reached Karachi so it was essential that we stay in close flight so that we could, if necessary, communicate by hand signals. If we had to force land in the desert we would need water, so we had to put bottles of water in any space available. We did not have even one complete set of aeronautical maps to cover the journey and would have to rely on picking up maps as we went along. Of great concern was the fact that of the twelve landing stages, only five would be likely to have RAF servicing facilities, and only one, Karachi, would be likely to have Hurricane servicing personnel and spares (hopefully!). We therefore had to consider the degree of unserviceability we would have to accept to continue the journey. For example, on the last leg of the journey from Toungoo to Rangoon, I took off knowing that I would be unlikely to raise my undercarriage or operate my flaps on landing, because of a fault in the hydraulic system. We had to then consider what we would be faced with when we arrived at Rangoon when we could be engaging enemy aircraft. We had had much training in identifying German and Italian aircraft and knowledge of the performance details of each aircraft. But we knew nothing about Japanese aircraft beyond what the Eagle (had it been published in 1941?) or its equivalent boys comic, might have known. We had heard however that the Japanese had a fighter in Burma, designated the Army 97, (the Zero forerunner) which was light, fast and very manoeuvrable. Finally, and of immediate concern, was that we would have to leave behind most of our personal possessions because of limited stowage space in the Hurricane. I thus left Cairo with no more than spare personal clothing which was stuffed in any available space; my flying log book along with other possessions, was left to follow on. Needless to say I never saw my logbook again. This is why, up to this time in my story, I have had to rely on memory as regards events and dates.

So off we set on our journey - six Hurricanes accompanied by a Blenheim bomber which was also off to Burma. We lined up on the airfield and individually went through the pre-take off check: 'Trim - set for take off, Mixture - fuel set for maximum power, Pitch - propeller blades set for maximum acceleration, Fuel - set for gravity feed from the reserve petrol tank, Flaps - set fully up'. Failure to apply each of these actions could have disastrous results.

Hence before and after every take off and landing Hurricane pilots would go through this drill, applying the varying settings as appropriate - TMPFF which I remembered by saying to myself 'Take Mary to the Pictures For a Frolic' (I tended to use a different word for the last F).

CHAPTER THREE

AIR DISPLAY FOR A SHEIK

I do not propose to detail the flight to Rangoon but will highlight some of the problems that occurred en route. In many respects the flights were enervating and boring. In fighting drowsiness I found that when necessary it was preferable to slide back the cockpit hood and regain alertness from both the rush of air passing by and over the cockpit, and the engine noise. But this could not be sustained for more than a few minutes at a time; I also had to make sure that I did not poke my head out otherwise it could have been head off; poor visibility through the heat haze was also a worrying factor.

On our first stop, Lydda, we were made aware that airfields on our route were likely to be too small for comfort in landing a Hurricane; this meant that our approaches and landings would have to be near to stalling speed if we could be assured of completing the landing run within the airfield boundary. This called for skilful landing - a difficult manoeuvre for inexperienced pilots. On the leg from Lydda to Habbaniya our navigation was helped by being able to follow, through the haze, an oil pipeline for some 400 miles. At Habbaniya there was an American B17 bomber (Flying Fortress), which after landing had gradually sunk in the sand due to its weight. It had been there some time as there was not a crane available that could lift or pull out such a heavy aircraft; I often wonder why and for how long it was there.

The real drama of the journey, as far as I was concerned, was landing at Bahrain in the Persian Gulf. Bahrain was a small airfield with no runways and subject to tidal flooding. A wall varying in height from, I believe, some one to two feet had been built to stop the sea encroaching onto the airfield; it would have been helpful if someone had told us this. Anyway, I approached the landing in a section of two, led by the squadron commander, and in open formation. My eyes were on his aircraft as we landed, with my Hurricane some thirty yards behind and to the right. I looked ahead on touchdown and congratulated myself on a smooth and safe landing. The next second all hell broke loose. I hit the wall, which I believe, was some two feet high at this point and hidden by drifting sand, at some 100mph; the undercarriage was ripped off, the nose of the aircraft tipped into the ground shattering the propeller and, if I recall correctly, the Hurricane somersaulted with bits breaking off leaving me at rest in a cockpit protected by the engine. On hitting the wall I had instinctively and fortunately turned off the fuel to reduce the risk of fire. I got out of the cockpit as quickly as I could and discovered that my only injury was three small cuts in the knuckles of my left hand which had protected my head as it crashed into the gunsight. How thankful I was to Sydney Camm for designing such a robust aircraft, which I believe, saved my life. I walked away from the crash, my hand wrapped in a handkerchief and after a minimum of fuss was presented to the Sheikh of Bahrain who was most excited by the air display he had witnessed and who regarded me as somewhat of a star. The squadron commander, upset that he had lost a Hurricane, was not in 'star worshipping' mood; he did however concede that the accident was not entirely my fault! Thank goodness post accident counsellors had not been invented to give me comfort, guidance and moral strength; the universities in those days had better things to do than churn out masses of sociologists!

The next day we set out for Sharjah with me as a passenger and cramped up in the gun turret of the Blenheim. Sharjah was interesting; because of problems with Arab terrorists and such like, the Hurricanes had to be taxied and pushed into the protective custody of a walled fort. The fort was not unlike those associated in our minds with Beau Geste and the French Foreign Legion.

We left Sharjah for Jiwani before dawn, hoping to complete the journey to Karachi that day. Jiwani turned out to be no more than a desert landing strip with a small WT station. There were no petrol stocks or refuelling bowsers and we waited some three - four hours for a camel train to arrive with petrol. The sight of some twenty camels, carrying drums of petrol approaching across the sand dunes was an incredible spectacle; slow, heavily laden camels bringing fuel for what were then high speed aircraft, was truly an anachronism I will always remember; even Hollywood might not believe it. The WT station did have two small hand carrying petrol pumps and we set about refuelling the Hurricanes. This involved pumping by hand some 1,400 gallons into the Hurricanes; no mean task for us in the heat of the midday sun, knowing that when we had done it there was still a three - four hour flight to get to Karachi. However, all went well and we landed at Karachi that day before sunset and without any dramas.

Karachi was an RAF station and one of the main bases of the RAF in India. Thus we knew that our aircraft would be thoroughly serviced but within the limitations that would apply to any servicing organisation ill equipped to service a modern aircraft such as the Hurricane. There were some servicing personnel from our squadron at Karachi who had come on by ship from Freetown; they worked hard on our aircraft but the spares situation limited their effectiveness.

Memories can be unreliable and often reinforced by exaggeration of the impressions gained from experiences and associated events. In my view of the RAF in India I may well have fallen into this trap. I thought they were in the main a smug, self satisfied and hostile lot who resented their comfortable life beginning to be disturbed by the war. In their defence, although the war had been going for two and a half years, they had had no opportunity of becoming involved, positioned as they were some 3,000 miles from Europe and the Middle East. The war against Japan had been going for some six weeks, but they did not have the aircraft that could effectively cope with the Japanese air threat. Aircraft such as Audaxes, Harts and Wapitis were first class bi-planes but their operational role was, and had been, limited to policing and maintaining order in the inter tribal hostilities of the North West Frontier and Afghanistan; this they did very effectively. I also felt that their pilots, who were mainly pre-war and experienced, resented that the Hurricanes were not available to them but were in the hands of comparatively inexperienced pilots such as ourselves. Anyway, one sensed certain undercurrent hostilities that manifested themselves accordingly. For example, the RAF in India had a standing instruction that all pilots arriving in India, and irrespective of their experience, had to be checked out in a dual control aircraft by an instructor before they were allowed to fly solo. This was a prudent rule bearing in mind that in normal times RAF pilots on arrival in India would have had four weeks leave, a six week boat trip, and could thus have had some three months without flying on arrival at their squadron. Sensible then to give them a dual check and the experience of flying over unfamiliar territory. But such a rule was not made for pilots flying in, in their single seat aircraft. However our squadron commander was informed by the station commander that before proceeding, each of our pilots would have to be checked out in a dual control aircraft; - was the station commander just being awkward? Our squadron commander refused to accept such an order, bearing in mind he had set out with instructions to get his squadron to Rangoon as soon as possible. Signals flashed to and from Air Headquarters Delhi and in the end common sense prevailed.

Another example was that on arrival, the Officers' Mess at Karachi was having a 'dining in' night; normal procedure in peacetime and once a week when all officers dined in wearing formal mess uniform. We only had what clothing we could carry in the Hurricane. Was it too much to expect that the Officers' Mess might receive us indifferently dressed and wish us well on our way? Not a bit of it; we were confined to our rooms and dinner was sent to us on a tray. But Karachi gave me a new lease of life, one of our pilots became sick, his Hurricane became available and so I was back in the fold.

From Karachi we flew on to Delhi. We now had radios but they were not very efficient and we could not raise the Delhi control tower. When we arrived over Delhi we were confronted by runways which were being extended and widened, and on which were some 300 coolies and two steamrollers. We flew low over the airfield flapping our wings and hoping it would dawn on them that we needed to land. Eventually they got the message and the runway was cleared apart from one of the steamrollers that appeared to have packed in. Unfortunately one of the Hurricanes hit the steamroller, damaging one of its wing tips. It was not fit to carry on and had to remain at Delhi until a spare wing tip could be flown in. However I must pay tribute to the station commander at Delhi. He was a wing commander who welcomed us enthusiastically and gave us every facility, which included dancing with his wife in a Delhi nightclub; she was quite dishy! On leaving for Allahabad the next morning we put on a short flying display in appreciation of his and his servicing crews' hospitality. At that time Delhi had a squadron of Valencia troop carrying aircraft. The Valencia was a large bi-plane that took off, cruised and landed at 65 - 70 mph. These aircraft had not been sent to Burma for obvious reasons, although they did play a significant part in evacuating personnel from Burma when the Japs advanced to the Indian border.

The trip to Calcutta via Allahabad was uneventful. The RAF airfield at Calcutta received us well and did all they could to prepare us for the following day when we were to set off for Burma. That night we were taken out to the infamous nightspots in Calcutta, which as far as I can remember had been enjoyable; I hope it was, as I had no money when I came to the next morning. However hangover or not, we left Calcutta bleary eyed on schedule. The aircraft had been given as thorough a servicing as was possible with limited facilities. The ammunition tanks had been filled and each one of the eight 303 Browning machine guns was cocked and ready for action. This meant leaving behind the more personal possessions because up until then the ammunition tanks had been space available for clothing etc.

We flew across the delta of the Brahmaputra and crossed the coast into Burma some 50 miles south of Chittagong. The terrain had now changed significantly; desert, semi-desert and some part cultivated ground had given way to thick jungle and ahead of us the 15,000 feet Chin Hills seemed to form a protective barrier against those wishing to penetrate into the main regions of Burma. The Chin Hills were also heavily jungled and it was apparent that an emergency forced landing would be out of the question; if faced with such an emergency the pilot would have to bale out and survival would become the problem. Faced with these conditions you took a close interest in how the engine was sounding; was the engine temperature OK? was the coolant system showing any signs of a possible leak? were the magnetos behaving themselves? was there plenty of fuel and was it being fed from the correct tanks? what about the oil pressure? While over the Chin Hills we fired our guns to check that they were loaded and working. We landed at Toungoo without mishap but I fancied that all was not right with my hydraulic system; it was slow to react which was particularly so with the flaps that had somewhat only reluctantly come down for landing. With the agreement of the squadron commander I decided that if necessary I would keep my undercarriage down on the final flight to Rangoon, hoping there was enough 'oomph' left in the hydraulic system to lower the flaps on landing. With the undercarriage down I had to fly at reduced speed so the others went ahead leaving me to follow on. I then became conscious that I was alone in a Hurricane which had limited speed and manoeuvrability, with the possibility that Japanese fighters might see this 'sitting duck'. I thought; to hell with it, and operated the undercarriage leaver; the undercarriage came up slowly but I was now fully manoeuvrable. I increased speed, and arrived at Mingaladon some fifteen minutes after the others. Mingaladon was to be our base and was just north of Rangoon. Before landing the undercarriage came down and locked under its own weight, and as the runway at Mingaladon was long I was able to land at increased speed without the flaps. This was the end of our journey and the end of the potential hazards that faced us when we left Cairo; but the sigh of relief on getting to Rangoon safely was to be overtaken by what we soon discovered was the impending drama of what was to be the losing battle to hold Burma.

We had arrived at Mingaladon towards the end of January 1942. Some of our ground crew had already arrived at Rangoon by sea and gave us a warm welcome. They took over our charges and in the next couple of days worked wonders in getting them as serviceable as they could bearing in mind limited spares, no workshops and no cover from the elements. Fortunately there had been a lull in Japanese air activity and we were able to get our accommodation organised. We established ourselves in a recently evacuated American Bible School some three miles from the airfield in a village called Insein. It was adequately appointed with kitchens and toilets; a classroom became our lounge and dining room and we found a suitable room for a bar which we stocked as a priority; the sleeping quarters were good and we found a gramophone with one record in good condition - 'Valse Triste'. All in all we felt that whatever the problems we might meet in the air, we would at least be able to return daily to reasonable comfort, in spite of the repetitive playing of 'Valse Triste'.

We were surprised to find that a squadron of the American Volunteer Guard (AVG) was operating from Mingaladon with their Tomahawk fighter planes - 'the Flying Tigers'. The AVG had been formed in, I believe, the mid to late '30s to reinforce the rather weak Chinese Air Force in what had become a long standing war with Japan. Their pilots were ex-US Army Air Force, very experienced and highly motivated by generous salaries and bonuses awarded for every Japanese aircraft destroyed. The AVG squadron had taken the full force of Japanese air attacks over Rangoon in late December and much of January, and their strength had been reduced to some dozen Tomahawks from which they were able to maintain roughly six for daily operations. Up to our arrival No 67 RAF Squadron, armed with Buffalo fighters which had flown up from Singapore, had been operating at Mingaladon but they had now been reduced to five Buffalos and withdrawn because of lack of spares and adequate servicing facilities. It was agreed to our mutual advantages that we operate when appropriate with the AVG. We also benefited tremendously from the help the AVG gave us in explaining Japanese air tactics and performance details of Japanese aircraft. In the next few weeks more Hurricanes arrived, but as I recall I do not believe we were ever able to put up a force at any one time of more than nine Hurricanes, and most of the time we were pushed to produce six aircraft.

We were tasked with the following operations: to defend these southern plains of Burma, and in particular Rangoon and the docks, from Japanese air attacks: to slow down the advancing Japanese army which had invaded north from Malaya through Thailand and was now within 100 miles of Rangoon across the Bay of Martaban: to give air support to the remnants of a British army which had valiantly fought a rearguard action north from Malaya and was attempting to stem the Japanese army while making preparations to get across the Sittang River into the lower plains of Burma and defend, in particular, Rangoon: to give fighter escort cover to a dwindling force of Blenheim bombers who were tasked with bombing Japanese strategic targets: and to attack on an opportunity basis the main Japanese air base at Moulmein from where most of the Japanese Air Force, both fighters and bombers, were now operating. To carry out these operations we had our small force of Hurricanes, the Tomahawks of the AVG, a dwindling force of Blenheim bombers, and an Indian squadron of Lysander aircraft which because of their specialised performance and role were limited in the help they could give.

We were some four - five weeks at Mingaladon and I suppose fighting a losing battle. During this period every pilot was in the air whenever serviceable aircraft were available; we all made an equal contribution and flew on average 35 operational hours each; most of these hours were flown in the latter two weeks. The breakdown of the various types of activity I was involved in was mirrored equally by the other pilots. My log book indicates: nine sorties escorting Blenheims attacking Japanese targets across the Salween; eight sorties attacking Japanese Army columns; six air defence sorties (two at night - another unforgettable experience); and three sorties attacking Moulmein airfield.

Our results were varied. In air defence we had little success mainly because what early warning system had existed was by now defunct and we were taking to the air too late. In fact on the two occasions I was 'shot up' by Japanese fighters I was climbing up to intercept when attacked from above. With a slower climbing speed a pilot is at a disadvantage against attacking aircraft diving at high speed from above; you cannot effectively attack and particularly if you are outnumbered, as we always seemed to be, you have to get away quickly and hope to get back to base with minimum damage.

In attacks against the Japanese Army we fared much better, leaving columns of destroyed and burning vehicles; I do not think we killed many troops, as they were able to disperse quickly into the jungle undergrowth. Some of the Japanese troops displayed great courage, standing their ground with a solitary rifle while facing an attack from an eight-gun Hurricane firing at the rate of 4,800 bullets per minute.

We believed that our attacks supporting the Blenheims, on towns such as Bilan and Kyaikto, met with a degree of success in giving our Army the opportunity to get across the Sittang River. On one occasion, to help the Army, we flew a maximum force of Blenheims, Tomahawks and Hurricanes, - some twenty five aircraft. As the Blenheims bombed, the Tomahawks strafed and, having established that no Jap fighters were around we, the escorting Hurricanes, followed up with further strafing attacks.

There had been a few attacks made on Moulmein airfield but with only small numbers of Hurricanes, the results had not really justified the risks. However on 24th February we mounted a maximum combined force of nine Hurricanes and six Tomahawks. We flew over the Bay of Martaban and caught the Japs by surprise. We had a field day, destroying many aircraft on the ground and a number in the air who were very vulnerable flying slowly while approaching to land. I was fortunate when on our return over the sea and while weaving and flying low to present a difficult target for the chasing Jap fighters, my propeller blades just clipped the sea surface. One foot lower at 320 mph and it could have been curtains. There was a vibration from the propeller and on landing I found each blade to be approximately one foot shorter with frayed ends. Tragically two of our pilots were killed on this raid and I believe the AVG lost one pilot. Other incidents come to mind. On one occasion a wounded Japanese pilot circled Mingaladon and dived at high speed at one of the Hurricanes on its landing run; he missed by no more than a few feet but made a mess of both himself and his aircraft. His body was found to have five bullets down the right hand side; he had preferred death and glory to limping back to his base.

The Army 97 fighter was armed only with two .28 low calibre machine guns: fortunately for us their bullets could not penetrate the 1/4" armour plate mounted to the rear of the Hurricane's cockpit. I was thankful for this when on one sortie I landed with two bullets embedded in the armour plate. If they had had .303 Browning machine guns with armour piercing bullets I would not have been writing this book.

Our combined and co-operative operations with the AVG worked well. We had mutual respect for each other and in recognition of the regard they had developed for the RAF they asked that Squadron Leader Frank Carey, the CO of No 17 Squadron, should lead the aforementioned attack on the Moulmein airfield. Our developing flying tactics recognised that while the Tomahawk was faster at the lower levels, the Hurricane was faster and more manoeuvrable at heights above 12,000 feet and particularly so at 20 - 25,000 feet. The Japanese Army 97 fighters were very manoeuvrable and fast because they were lightly constructed, carried no protective armour plate, and only mounted two machine guns. The Japanese paid little regard for the safety of their pilots.

To our dismay Singapore fell on 14th February, and towards the end of February what was left of the AVG were withdrawn to China. They had fought bravely and suffered many casualties in defending Rangoon against the mass raids of the Japanese in late December and early January. To our sorrow we heard later that due to engine failure some had failed to reach China. We were ordered to fly north in what Hurricanes we still had and as and when they became serviceable. On 27th February two of us (I believe we were the last) took off for Magwe, an airfield on the Irrawady some 100 miles south of Mandalay. Pilots who had no aircraft, and the ground crew, were left to set fire to the no longer flyable Hurricanes and to destroy all equipment and supplies and then head north to Prome, in all available transport.

The evening before leaving for Magwe two of us had wandered onto the golf course at Insein. Because of the impending arrival of the Japanese, the population had been rushing to get away and the professional's shop and clubhouse had been abandoned. We treated ourselves to a beer and, with new clubs, hit a few balls ineffectively: fifty five years later I am still hitting golf balls ineffectively! That night at Magwe we learnt that the pilots and ground crews of 136 Squadron who had been left in India were now reforming at Akyab, an island south of the Arakan, having been equipped with replacement Hurricanes. Akyab and the Arakan were to be the last British foothold in Burma. While at Magwe I recall meeting with General Alexander who had arrived in Burma from the UK to put order and discipline into the likely retreat from Burma; he had been the General who had masterminded the Dunkirk operation. I recall he wanted to know the latest position at Rangoon. I thought him a most impressive officer and leader who by his manner inspired confidence. The following day our section of two flew back across the Chin Hills and landed at Akyab and were delighted to meet up with the bulk of the pilots and ground crews of 136 Squadron, who were making preparations to oppose an impending Japanese air and ground attack.

The squadron had been given adequate numbers of Hurricane replacements but they were only Hurricane Mk 1s and each aircraft log had, written in red, 'unfit for operations'. Since being withdrawn from operations they had been flogged to death in training establishments and had outflown their useful service life. It was believed that en route from Karachi the Mk 2 Hurricanes earmarked for us in Burma had been swapped by interested parties for these old 'past it' aircraft, and rumour led us to believe that Karachi, not my most favourite RAF station, was not entirely innocent.

Akyab was a commercial centre for trading, with its large dockyard and entrepreneurial population, which was mainly Indian. There had been little air activity before we arrived in early March and patrolling over the sea in search of Japanese shipping was initially our main task. I recall on two occasions we spotted a surfaced submarine but we had no intelligence information to identify whether it was friend or foe; so we had to watch while it submerged. Much later when we arrived back in Calcutta it became apparent when talking to Naval intelligence that they would have been Japanese. The main Akyab airfield was dangerously near to the town and dockyards so we moved our operational base to a small satellite strip, which for some reason was named 'Old Angus'. During this lull intelligence indicated that the Japanese would soon be turning their attention to Akyab and the Arakan with the aim of completing their takeover of the whole of Burma.

The blitz came on the 23rd and 24th March. On both these days Akyab and the docks were attacked by large formations of Japanese bombers with fighter escorts. It would, I believe, be misleading to convert memories of general and personal experiences to factual events and statistics. I am talking about a maximum of roughly fifteen - twenty clapped out Hurricanes attempting to attack waves of bombers being protected by formations of some twenty, fifty, one hundred? - who knows - Japanese fighters. They covered the sky like swarms of mosquitoes. In the ensuing one-sided air battles we claimed some ten kills and many probables. But in effect we were shot out of the air and it was a miracle that of the seven Hurricanes shot down, all but one of our pilots survived having either baled out or force landed. It was gratifying and comforting to know that in spite of the shambles those pilots injured had received prompt medical treatment, and had been flown by DC2 aircraft to hospital in Calcutta. I should add here that the Valencia squadron from Delhi, played a significant role in assisting the evacuation of troops etc from Burma to India in spite of their vulnerability.

After the raids on the 24th March it was realised that our depleted force of Hurricanes, some half dozen, which were flyable but not really fit for operations could have no effective influence on the war in Burma and the order came through to withdraw. Although my aircraft had suffered damage, I was OK and on 26th March four of us flew off to Chittagong in India. We then set off for Calcutta but had to return to Chittagong because of bad weather. We took off for Calcutta the next day and landed at Dum Dum, some ten miles from Calcutta. My Hurricane by now was in a sorry state and I flew it to a newly established Maintenance Unit and left it there. It was the same Hurricane that I had flown from Karachi, and which had looked after me in Rangoon and Akyab. It may sound stupid but I had moments of regret that we were parting.

At Calcutta I reflected. We had initially expected to fly off HMS Ark Royal to relieve Malta; the carrier had been sunk and we were off to the Caucasus. At Freetown with Japan now in the war, it was decided that we would divert to Takoradi and fly our Hurricanes to Rangoon. At Takoradi we found that our Hurricanes had been taken over by the Middle East Air Force and we reached Cairo by PAN AM Airways. At Cairo we were the 'piggy in the middle' in disagreements between Middle East Command and the Chiefs of Staff's Committee in London, as to whether we fly on to Rangoon or not. The flight from Egypt to Burma had presented problems: airfields with short runways; no radio communications; no navigation aids and shortage of maps; limited, and at some bases no servicing facilities; lack of spares; problems compounded when faced by inexperienced pilots. In Rangoon we had flown and fought hard although our achievements had had little impact on the war in Burma, apart from hopefully saving some lives and at best giving the Japanese a bloody nostril. The defence of Akyab had been a forlorn hope with the odds against us.

The foregoing is not a criticism of our masters who were conducting the war effort. Great Britain, with the Commonwealth, was having to fight on all fronts with no support at all except from the Americans, who in the first few months of 1942 had their hands full stemming the Japanese advance in the Pacific. It is unbelievable we seem to have forgotten that the U.S.A. was our only ally in the war which saved Europe, if not the world. Except for the valiant efforts of such as the Norwegians, Fins and European partisan groups, the European countries did nothing to help.

CHAPTER FOUR

THE RED ROAD RUNWAY

In Calcutta chaos reigned along with panic based on a belief that the Japanese might arrive at any moment. The refugees that poured in from Burma could not be readily accommodated and were living on the streets. In order to get quickly to safer areas they, along with many indigenous Bengalis, were leaving by every train available, and there were as many passengers on the roofs and footboards as there were in the carriages; not a few suffered death or injury falling on to the line. Dead bodies in the streets were not an unusual sight; disfigured and emaciated beggars hounded the passers-by; cockroaches thrived; rats were risking daylight scavenging, and the conglomerate of smells in what was the hottest summer in Calcutta for some seventy years, was indescribable.

To help to understand much of what follows I need to outline the structure and organisation of the squadron. Typically a fighter squadron was commanded by a squadron leader and had eighteen aircraft, approximately thirty - thirty five pilots, two hundred ground personnel to service the aircraft, comprising fitters, riggers, armourers, radio mechanics and miscellaneous trades such as clerks, cooks, drivers, medical staff, police etc. The operational structure was centred on two Flights, A & B, each commanded by a flight lieutenant. Each flight had nine aircraft, some fifteen pilots and first line servicing crews headed by a flight sgt. An engineering officer was responsible for all the servicing including major and minor inspections and also for the fleet of mechanical transport. An adjutant assisted the squadron commander in administration; a medical officer and an intelligence officer completed the complement. The total number of personnel could depend on location and other considerations, but generally would be between 200 - 300.

On the flying side the minimum unit comprised a section of two aircraft, - a leader and his No 2, - for mutual protection; in the event of the leader engaging an enemy, the task of the No 2 was to protect the leader. Two sections comprising four aircraft were led by the senior in experience of the two section leaders . . . and so on. Although overall loyalty was to the squadron, there was a strong loyalty to each Flight from both pilots and ground crews. Until I became a squadron commander, I made sure that regardless of what squadron I was in, I was in the B Flight; to me B Flight were action men and A Flight were poofs.

Our orders were to reform as a squadron at Alipore, an airfield near to Calcutta used by the Bengal Flying Club. Work had already started to lengthen the runway and it was hoped that the surfaces would be sufficiently strong to support Hurricane operations. But how to get a squadron organised in such a complex and confusing situation? The whereabouts of the majority of 136 Squadron personnel who had not been in Burma were generally unknown; they were dispersed throughout India helping to service Hurricanes and other aircraft coming east, to strengthen what had now become the defence of India. Time was of the essence and so the squadron sent signals to all RAF stations and units ordering them to arrange for all 136 Squadron personnel to immediately re-join the squadron in Calcutta. These signals short circuited the RAF administrative structure and cut across the chain of command; but they got results. Personnel started arriving by train, air and boat; they included some pilots who had been keeping in flying practice in the north-west frontier. Eight Hurricanes, with pilots and ground crew that had been sent to Ceylon to oppose a threat from the Japanese Navy, were relieved and flown to Alipore. The British Army provided vehicles and much essential equipment such as tents and huts needed to support airfield operations. Our airmen showed great initiative by purchasing locally items not readily available from Service sources; these included items such as screwdrivers and a sewing machine (for patching up the central fuselage fabric of a Hurricane). Blackboards were borrowed from a local school, to show the ever changing states of readiness of aircraft, pilots and ground crews. Accommodation was a problem; the airmen were accommodated in a 'seen better days' maharajah's palace, while the NCOs and officers were booked into two hotels in the centre of Calcutta. Additional Hurricanes were flown in and in a short time the squadron was roughly complete with approximately 22 Hurricanes, 30 pilots and some 2 - 300 ground personnel. The squadron crest, a Woodpecker, was painted on all our aircraft and vehicles and this helped to establish our identity and presence in Calcutta. Our pilots in hospital were able to re-join us; two having recovered from severe burns and one from facial injuries. The latter gave us great amusement by recounting the difficulty he had when in the sea, in trying to blow up his Mae West with two bullet holes in his cheek. Two of these pilots were to be killed a year later in combat operations when we returned to Burma.

In spite of the foregoing difficulties the squadron was able to be declared 'operational', and my log book tells me that within two weeks of my arrival in Calcutta from Burma, I, with three others was patrolling south of Diamond Harbour waiting to intercept a reported impending air attack on Calcutta docks. A number of British families offered friendship and hospitality and provided canteen and such like facilities. But in case I've given the impression that Calcutta had come together in the sort of spirit evidenced in the London blitz, I must say that Ghandi's 'British quit India' and civil disobedience campaigns were already having adverse effects, in turning much of the Indian population against the British. The Indian Army and Air Force were very loyal but there was more than talk about the forming of a separate Indian Army, which would join with the Japanese when they invaded. Fighting, when you are not sure of your friends, does not help morale.

Although preparations were being made to resist an imminent attack by the Japanese by land, sea and air, such an attack did not materialise. Intelligence information on Japanese strengths and movements in Burma was virtually non-existent, but it became apparent that Japan's success in taking over the whole of Burma had overstretched their resources. A serious attempt to invade India could not be contemplated by them until they had paused to receive reinforcements and re-group, and the next few months saw both sides making limited gestures such as hit and run tactics. This meant that we had to be continually on our toes, holding aircraft in a state of readiness and, because of a lack of an effective early warning system, having to scramble and intercept what generally turned out to be friendly aircraft. Any serious attempt by the Japanese Air Force to mount a bombing attack on Calcutta and the docks was met by an ever-strengthening fighter defence, which resulted in the Japs turning back before reaching their target.

In effect we settled into what became a tiring and debilitating routine. Our aircraft had to be dispersed every evening so as not to present a vulnerable target to night bombing. This meant at dusk flying them to what were virtually strips of flat ground and lashing them down (a monsoon storm could easily toss a Hurricane over). Then an hour before dawn, driving out to the strips, unlashing the aircraft and then flying them back to Alipore. We were able to disperse some aircraft by taxiing them along roads and housing them in bamboo shelters. However some of the shelters had a low doorway height and a Hurricane could only enter when the propeller blades were not in a vertical position. So having switched off the engine we would wait for a team of airmen to arrive to help push the Hurricane under cover. On one occasion I tried to taxi my aircraft into a hut, which I thought had sufficient propeller clearance. My propeller hit the roof, and so did the squadron commander when he ended up with an aircraft grounded while awaiting a replacement propeller. The three hours taken to disperse and recover the aircraft every dusk and dawn extended what was already a long day. It was difficult staying alert all day in the heat and maintaining a state of readiness. We started suffering from colds and skin infections. We would take off in temperatures over 100F with 98% humidity and in sweaty flying overalls, only to find that at 30,000 feet the unpressurised cockpits and sweaty overalls were icing up in the intense cold; and so were we! The conditions resulted in all of us suffering prickly heat rash and a more intimate rash, - dhobi itch, - caused by poorly laundered garments. Diarrhoea was something we came to live with, resulting from the lack of hygiene in food growing, handling and cooking. Diarrhoea is often seen as solely discomforting but the type we suffered from went further; we had one death and cases of ruined stomachs, - collapse of lining, ulcers etc.

Although the Army and the RAF were beginning to receive reinforcements they were still comparatively weak. However there was a need to show the Japs that we could take the offensive and in late May we were tasked with flying east to Chittagong and Arakan and to engage any Jap aircraft on an opportunity basis. However, our first efforts to carry out such sorties coincided with the beginning of the monsoons. A feature of the monsoons was the build up of cumulo nimbus cloud formations with the classical anvil type heads, and these were already becoming evident over the Sunderbands (the approx. 200 mile wide delta of the Ganges) between Calcutta and Chittagong. These clouds could tower from a base of 1,000 feet up to over 40,000 feet; the cloud core developed the up currents which could take over an aircraft, suck it up out of control and spit it out, damaged, at the top. To reinforce the point, a year or two later a squadron of approx sixteen Spitfires flew into a cu nimb and was virtually destroyed. The precise details are now vague in my mind but the tragedy was of the order of three pilots crashing and being killed, five pilots baling out, four crash landing but surviving and four finding alternative airfields to land on. Having talked about the dangers of the weather, on our first two attempts to cross the Sunderbands we lost two aircraft, not due to the weather but because of the failure of locally manufactured spares such as rubber joints connecting up the coolant system. I witnessed a colleague spring a glycol leak and within seconds he had gone out of control and crashed to his death. Another Hurricane also had to force land but the pilot survived. However, these sorties were good for our morale as we felt that the Japanese Air Force had by now little enthusiasm for seeking engagements with RAF fighters on the offensive. One or two fighter squadrons were now beginning to reinforce our still meagre fighter force but the problem was now lack of airfields. And so an incredible but imaginative and practical decision was made to use a road, the Red Road, in the middle of Calcutta, as an airfield; and as we were now regarded as an experienced squadron we were ordered to be the first to operate from this bizarre airfield.

The Red Road ran parallel with, and some two hundred yards from Chowringee, the main road in the centre of Calcutta. If Chowringee was Oxford Street, then the Red Road was the equivalent of the Mall. The road was cambered and about the width of the 'wing tip to wing tip' span of a Hurricane; on either side was a strip of grass some fifteen feet wide and each edged with a decorative stone balustrade, which was higher than the wing tip of a Hurricane. Beyond the balustrades were trees and our dispersal and operating area for the aircraft was amongst the trees between the Red Road and Chowringee. At the town centre end of the Red Road was a roundabout with a statue (I believe this was Queen Victoria) and beyond the roundabout the road extended into a busy, congested street. Our problem was to approach over the statue at a minimum speed above stalling, and land the Hurricane as near to the end as possible to ensure we did not run out of road. The last building we would pass over on the approach to landing was, as I remember, the Great Eastern Hotel and we had a duty pilot on its flat roof who would fire a red or green verey light according to whether, in his opinion, we were too low or too high or just at the right height for landing. It was important to land along the middle line of the road, otherwise the camber could edge the Hurricane to one side; this could result in a wing tip getting caught on the balustrade wall which in turn could swing the aircraft around through 90° crashing it into the wall. Such an event at high speed would demolish a forty foot length of wall; at low speed it demolished a smaller length of wall penetrated by the propeller and engine. We were to fly off the Red Road from the 26th June to 5th September 1942, - some ten weeks; when we moved there were I believe two large gaps in the walls and a few little gaps! For safety reasons we tried to have the balustrades removed, along with the statue, but 'intelligence' said that the Japs could cotton on to the fact that we were using the Red Road as an airfield - thinks - so what? The 'intelligence' branches of the Services played a vital role in the war but I did think, as in this case, that the term 'intelligence' was not always appropriate to cover all their activities.

My most vivid memory of flying off the Red Road was one day when I was landing in the direction towards Queen Victoria (an unusual landing direction and against the normally prevailing wind). My brakes were poor and I had them fully on while approaching the roundabout and its statue. When I reached the roundabout my speed allowed me to skid around it without the undercarriage collapsing and I crashed through a bamboo type fencing and came to rest between two trams and surrounded by what appeared to be the whole population of Calcutta! Fortunately nobody was hurt, the aircraft was intact and a multitude of hands helped to push the Hurricane back through the gap in the bamboo fence.

Hurricane landing on the Red Road in centre of Calcutta, July 1942

In early May the officers left the Grand Hotel and were accommodated in an extremely pleasant villa in the suburbs of Calcutta. It was shortly after this that a strange episode occurred. It was late at night and two of us were chatting on the veranda, having enjoyed a few bevies, when we saw a flashlight coming from a nearby house. It became readily apparent that some morse code communication was taking place and as it was past midnight the circumstances were, to say the least, suspicious. We woke some of the others and armed with our .38 revolvers made a beeline for the building climbing over various obstacles in our way. When we got to the building the light was still transmitting so we crashed in, guns at the ready, and found on the top floor an office with two or three Bengalis, a signalling lamp, and what we thought were code books;

one of the Bengalis was armed. They claimed they were bookmakers signalling the odds on certain horses entered in the Calcutta races the next day. The squadron commander then appeared wondering what the hell we were doing and immediately contacted the Provost Marshal. When the military police arrived, we withdrew. Later that day the Provost Marshal contacted our CO and sent a message congratulating us for having caught what appeared to be members of a spy ring who were now under arrest. We were relieved that alcohol had not led us to make fools of ourselves. The monsoon broke over Calcutta in mid June. It was a relief to stand out and freshen up in the heavy rain, but after every storm the heat and humidity returned with increased intensity. We now understood why the British in India took to the hills during the monsoons, and, war or no war, most were not going to remain in Calcutta. The hill stations were at attractive locations such as for example, Darjeeling, Simla, Kashmir; they were expensive to stay at and generally beyond the financial means of servicemen even on short leaves.

In July, Ghandi's 'British quit India' and civil disobedience campaigns gained a momentum and we experienced the beginnings of open hostility to the British. (I believe Ghandi was visiting Calcutta at the time). Ghandi's policy was passive resistance but once a crowd forms and gets stirred up, the militant hot heads soon take control and hysteria results. There were incidents involving British servicemen; one evening on leaving a cinema a soldier a few feet away from me had his arm slashed open by an Indian who quickly disappeared into the crowd; this was not an isolated incident. Intelligence reports indicated that the Hurricanes on the Red Road could be vulnerable to attacks and/or sabotage and for a few days all squadron personnel went armed with rifles and guns and worked a shift system maintaining a 24 hour guard. On one night a very hostile crowd gathered in Chowringee and two Hurricanes were brought forward with guns sighted to fire over their heads, as a last resort to deter an attack. Fortunately such a measure did not become necessary.

In August, 'intelligence' reported that Japanese bombers were believed to be starting or planning to start operations from the Andaman Islands, with the aim of attacking our shipping in the Bay of Bengal. We were ordered to position a flight of some eight Hurricanes at Vizagapatan, some 600 miles south of Calcutta on the east coast. Our orders were to patrol the sea areas in the hope of intercepting such bombers. But there was no radar or radio location network and no air to ground communication, so we had to maintain a section of two Hurricanes in the air all the time in the vain hope that we would make a visual interception. During the ten days we were there we sighted a Japanese flying boat, which immediately dropped its bombs, entered clouds and was never seen again!

After returning from Vizagapatan the squadron was moved from the Red Road to Dum Dum airfield north of Calcutta. It may be cocky to say but the squadron that replaced us at the Red Road managed, in a very short time, to increase considerably the number of gaps in the balustrade walls! The move to Dum Dum meant moving out of the comfortable villa in Calcutta and taking over penny packets of dispersed sub standard accommodation; our airmen regretted having to leave their maharajah's palace. It's of interest to note that Dum Dum airfield was named after the nearby factory that had manufactured the infamous soft nosed dum dum bullets.

The Japanese Air Force was now beginning to flex its muscles in Burma and was sending the occasional bomber formations to attack Bengal and in particular Calcutta and its docks. However, our fighter strength was building up (I believe by September 1942 we had five squadrons in the area totalling some 80 - 100 aircraft). We were now able to scramble larger numbers of Hurricanes to repel these raids, which meant that the Japs were again turning back when short of their targets.

Although this meant that we were successfully defending the area, it was frustrating not to have the opportunity of intercepting and engaging the enemy. Indeed, I believe that throughout 1942 only three bombers penetrated our defences over Calcutta; these came by night and dropped bombs at random before scuttling back, having achieved negligible bomb damage on the ground. We were technically day fighters but we did operate when necessary at night in vain attempts to intercept an enemy bomber; without radar or other target location means we were on a losing wicket. However the fact of our presence in the air was normally sufficient to deter the Japanese from penetrating into the area.

There were now rumours that the Army in the Arakan was being strengthened and that we would be moving back to Chittagong to give them ground support and air protection. Our training hours increased and in particular included practising very low flying, air to ground diving attacks, and aerial combat coupled with improving our ability to individually take the Hurricane through more technically demanding manoeuvres, flying it to its limits, to ensure our superiority against the Japanese Zero fighters. Tail chasing, aerobatics, dog fighting, high-speed low level manoeuvres became the order of the day. The dangers of such intensive training are real and during the six month period ending mid December 1942, five squadron pilots were killed without help from the Japanese.

One of many of our problems operating from Dum Dum was that, as with Alipore, the Hurricanes had to be dispersed at night and hidden in bamboo shelters. But at Dum Dum this meant taxiing along busy roads in the dark and avoiding, particularly at dawn, the farmers taking their produce and animals to market. The engine in a Hurricane cuts out any forward vision, and steering a Hurricane with your head sticking out of the cockpit to one side trying to see ahead in the dark, with chickens, goats, Uncle Tom Cobley and all, is not without its hazards. Wonderful material for the Ealing comedy series of films of the 50s and 60s.

But life at Dum Dum was not without its dramas. Operating from an increasingly hostile environment was to say the least unnerving. Many, particularly those airmen who had left wives and children at home, were beginning to question why we were there; many felt they were fighting for a country more loyal to the Hindu rabble rouser Ghandi, or to the emerging Moslem leader Jinnah, than to its own government. Sickness rates and skin complaints increased; the heat, humidity, poor food, indifferent living conditions, the poor quality of locally produced spares, the boring 'readiness routine' and training commitments all added to the frustrations of not being able to get to grips with the enemy; an enemy that we all knew had to be defeated if we were to return to our families in the UK. Cases of indiscipline arose and had to be dealt with, and as I was now a deputy flight commander, I had to face up to the problems of man management. On one occasion I was appointed to the Board of three officers of a field Court Martial, to pass judgement on one of our two flight commanders who had been charged with conduct prejudicial to good order and discipline. We, the Board, found him guilty and he was reprimanded and posted away from the squadron. But when I look back I wonder whether those who had brought about his Court Martial, had not themselves been guilty of triggering off unnecessary action against an officer who, although a bit of a hot head, had the courage of his convictions and the guts to regard his personal safety as less important than defeating an enemy. There was also emerging an undercurrent of ill feeling from the commissioning, before we left England, of some sergeant pilots. The need for increasing the complement of officers had been because, in addition to exercising responsibilities in the air, a squadron, particularly one going overseas, could not effectively operate and administer itself without a structured proportion and balance between the numbers of officers to the other ranks. The officer complement had therefore to be increased, with newly commissioned officers being given various administrative responsibilities in addition to those in the air. But experience throughout 1942 indicated that not all those newly commissioned officers had developed the professional flying ability and leadership qualities to earn the respect of their peers. And thus pragmatic decisions were having to be made, which could result on occasions in a sergeant pilot leading a section in the air with an officer as his number two.

Additionally, some of our new pilot replacements were experiencing difficulties being accepted into the core of the original and, by now, more experienced squadron pilots; this was our own fault but nevertheless true.

Coming back to myself, during this period I succumbed to sand fly fever which only lasted for some seven days but left me somewhat weak. Sand fly fever was a sort of less severe complaint than its dreaded companion - malaria.

But in bringing 1942 towards an end I must say that the foregoing was typical of the day to day frustrations that come to the fore when there is insufficient satisfying work to meet the needs of, in this case, those wanting to see a satisfactory end to the war. Overall, there was little that could not be put right by a return to more intensely active operations and the chance to vent those frustrations on the Japanese. And this chance arose when on 21st December 1942 the squadron was ordered to its new base at Chittagong.

CHAPTER FIVE

DUSTING THE GENERAL

The squadron move to Chittagong on 21st December 1942 had been preceded by a build up of Japanese air and ground activity in both the North Burma and Arakan areas. In early December we, along with 135 Squadron, had been sent to the Arakan area to test the temperature, - the extent and effectiveness of the Japanese air activity. We soon realised that the threat was not based on Japanese bluff. Their Army 97 and 01 fighter aircraft were there in plenty and starting to be replaced with the 'Zeros'. They were flying with the same fanatical zeal and dedication to serve their Emperor as we had seen earlier at Rangoon. We gave air cover protection to Blenheims and Lysanders on tactical bombing raids and attacked Japanese ground troops being engaged by the British Army; we also went on the offensive in defending Chittagong and its environs from bombing raids. These operations were not intensive; as I remember we accounted for some three Japanese fighters and two bombers while losing four Hurricanes; two of these Hurricanes were from our squadron with the pilots surviving, while the other two involved fatalities suffered by 135 Squadron.

So we set off to establish our base at Chittagong conscious that the next few months could be critical to the future outcome of the war. The Middle East situation, though improved from the state it was in early 1942, was still critically poised and the possibility of the Germans advancing through Persia and the Gulf and meeting up in India with Japanese forces, who might by then have overrun India, was not beyond the bounds of possibility. Thus I think, looking back, that we were all conscious of the importance of successfully re-entering Burma to forestall any advance by the Japanese into India. We knew the fighting would be tough; retreat back to Calcutta would be out of the question; and in a nutshell it would be 'shit or bust'. I believe our mental attitude to facing the inevitable fighting ahead of us was positive and determined. But I, along with some of the others, approached the re-entry to Burma in a markedly different frame of mind from that which I had on arrival at Rangoon a year earlier. Then, I was somewhat naive, aware of my limited flying experience but with an over-confident belief in my ability to survive and a conviction that I was somewhat blessed with immortality, - a belief that it would always happen to the other chap! Since then, following my experiences in our retreat from Burma, and the intensity of the training we had undertaken in Calcutta in re-building and preparing the squadron for operations, I had certainly grown up and developed a more mature approach to facing the uncertainties of the future. I had come to realise the importance of experience in looking after myself and those I would be responsible for when on flying operations; experience which made you realise the need to fly within the limits of your aircraft and your flying ability; experience which made one realise that each of us had a duty to improve our flying and fighting abilities for mutual support, protection and effectiveness in aerial combat. My thoughts had turned to aspects of leadership for I had now been appointed as the deputy flight commander of B Flight. I thus had responsibility not only for myself but also for others; to try to ensure that they were not exposed to irresponsible actions which could result in not only fatalities and injuries, but in the loss of aircraft that were still in short supply. I was coming to realise that leadership in the air when immediate decisions were needed, had to be based on experience and 'onus' in doing instinctively what you believed was right, while leaving the outcome to decide, perhaps at times unfairly, the extent to which you were either a good or bad leader. Finally it could be thought that the foregoing amounts to ensuring that I put personal safety and safety for others, as a priority. Any pilot who followed such a doctrine would be displaying cowardice. In war an aggressive spirit is essential; risks have to be taken; injury or death have to be expected but not seen as necessarily inevitable.

An advance party of ground personnel had been flown ahead to Chittagong to receive the aircraft, while the main squadron party was already on its way by train and depending on conditions a combination of train and boat; a small rear party was left to see us off. This may sound as though these moves were straightforward, but travel in India in those days had its hazards and it was solely due to the administration and planning by the squadron headquarters staff, which ensured that we all arrived at the same place and roughly when expected.

When we arrived over Chittagong one of the Flights stayed in the air to give protection to the other Flight that had landed and was refuelling. This precaution was in anticipation that the Japs might be attacking us, because it was one of those occasions when 'Tokyo Rose' had made reference to the hot reception that the 'Woodpecker' Squadron would receive if it returned to the Arakan. ('Tokyo Rose' was the Japanese equivalent of Germany's 'Lord Haw Haw'). However the Japs did not appear so our attention turned to the problem of accommodation: there was none. Yes, - dispersal huts had been constructed on the airfield to support flying operations and living accommodation huts were being constructed for the ground crew, but they were not yet ready and no thought appeared to have been given to SNCO and officer living accommodation. So we all, - officers, pilots and ground crew - took over an abandoned Indian village of mud huts, - no windows, low openings for doors, no floor coverings; the only furniture was charpoys (bamboo and rope beds) housing creepy crawlies ready to attack. A field kitchen was quickly organised to feed us all. The ground crews moved by stages into their newly constructed bamboo huts, while the pilots and officers moved temporarily into billets in Chittagong town some fifteen miles away. However to complete the accommodation story the powers that be considered that the travel to and from Chittagong was using up too much petrol, so back we came to the abandoned, mud-hutted Indian village. We found some old dilapidated huts which although full of muck we felt would be preferable to the mud huts; we set about cleaning them out and they became our living quarters. These living conditions were unacceptable to support pilots on daily flying operations so following sustained pressure, particularly from our commanding officer, we were authorised after some four weeks to return to the billets in Chittagong.

Before outlining our operational tasks I need to explain the state of the war as it was in Burma and the Arakan. The Arakan was a heavily jungled strip of land running south from Chittagong; it was bordered by the Chin Hills to the east and by the Bay of Bengal to the west. The northern area of the Arakan was part of India, the southern area being in Burma; the division came approximately fifty miles north of Akyab Island, which had been our last air base before we retreated from Burma. Now at that time the British Army had advanced a few miles into the area, which was Burma and was some forty miles from Akyab. The army's aim was to take Akyab and, as resources allowed, advance further south down the Arakan to take over other bases occupied by the Japanese such as Ramree Island. There were no other hostilities taking place in Burma except that the first Chindit Expedition under General Wingate had recently set out to penetrate into northern Burma and to demonstrate the practicalities of the long-range penetration technique. The role of the RAF was to support the army by winning and maintaining air superiority over the whole area of operations and to give direct ground support to the fighting army units. Briefly the RAF strength in the Arakan was now some four fighter squadrons and a small force of Blenheim bombers and Lysanders. The fighter squadrons had flown with us during the build up in the Calcutta area, and just before leaving for Burma we had flown with them as a 53 aircraft 'wave the flag' formation over Calcutta, for the Viceroy of India and to bolster the morale of the population. So the squadrons all saw themselves as part of a team. Also in spite of the accommodation problems and the varying sicknesses we had come to expect living in poor conditions, the morale of the squadron personnel was high with an enthusiasm to get stuck into the Japs. The types of operations we were to become involved with included air to air and air to ground attacks on enemy aircraft, escorting our bombers and troop carrying aircraft, direct strafing of enemy front line troops, and long range penetration sorties across the Chin Hills into central Burma attacking either planned or opportunity targets.

We were involved in some of these operations within 24 hours of arriving in Chittagong, including direct air support of the army, repelling air attacks against Chittagong and other bases housing our forces. It soon became apparent that whereas we were going in search of Japanese fighters, they tended to be more defensive. I believe they realised that the Army 01 fighter was

Three of the senior pilots, Kit, Connie and Joe

Pilots at Chittagong awaiting call to readiness

Kit with his fitter and rigger

Refuelling and rearming after combat

inferior to the 8 gun Hurricanes as flown by the RAF pilots. (The Zeros had not yet appeared in significant numbers). However they were far from sitting ducks and, with their fanatical faith in their Emperor, would when cornered press home an attack with complete disregard for their safety, - the Kamikaze touch!

Within a week of arriving at Chittagong our new squadron commander went missing believed killed (he had replaced Squadron Leader Elsdon who had been promoted to wing commander and was now leader of the wing comprising Nos. 135, 136 and 17 Squadrons). The squadron commander with his No 2, had been flying low over the sea and approaching to attack aircraft on Akyab airfield. It was dawn, the sea was smooth and with patches of mist it was difficult to judge height accurately. His aircraft hit the sea going at some 300mph. His No 2 circled the spot but could see no trace of him or any debris. Five days later he arrived by truck at our airfield, with a broken nose but otherwise physically intact. He had surfaced after the crash buoyed by his Mae West, seen his No 2 flying off and some time later had been picked up by some native fishermen. They had hidden him in their village and then passed him up the coast by fishing boat and lastly bullock cart. The Army had then brought him back by truck. They were indeed brave fishermen and villagers; had the Japs known any of this they would all have been executed.

The problem now facing us, his brother officers, was that he wondered what could have happened to some of his personal possessions that had not been packaged up for return to the UK; personal possessions such as 400 cigarettes, bottles of booze and such like. We all reacted by sheepishly also wondering what could have happened to them! It may seem callous but whenever a pilot was killed, the others would rush to his room to grab any perishable goods (there's a smoking boozy animal in all of us!). It was felt that he could not continue in his post as squadron commander, because his safety and that of those who had helped him to get back would be put at risk were he to fall subsequently into enemy hands. We were sorry to see him go and some three weeks later welcomed our new squadron commander. He was an experienced pilot having been in the Battle of Britain and he was readily accepted by all; particularly as one of his first actions was to get the RAF Group Commander to approve the pilots vacating their filthy accommodation by the airfield and moving back to the town of Chittagong.

Many of the operations we would be called upon to fly would take us beyond the range of a Hurricane flying solely on internal petrol tanks. The long-range tanks we had used to extend our range when flying from Egypt to Rangoon had been fixed to the aircraft and could not be jettisoned. The Hurricanes and tanks had now been modified so that the tanks could be jettisoned by the pilot in flight, and the aircraft become fully manoeuvrable. Thus we could now fly to a target up to some 250 miles away, jettison the tanks if necessary, engage in operations and have sufficient fuel to return to base.

We also now had flying overalls that were lightweight but gave protection from fire in the cockpit. Unfortunately they could not solve the problem we still faced of being in the extreme cockpit heat at low level and climbing to the freezing conditions at 30,000 feet. We also now carried a .38 revolver, a machete to chop our way back through the jungle, a survival kit compromising first aid equipment, umpteen different tablets and a hard tack biscuit. When flying over enemy territory we now wore a belt strapped around our waist and holding 100 gold coins, to use as necessary in seeking native help for survival. After a time, when the 'bandits', as against the more peaceful and law abiding villagers, came to know of the gold we wondered whether that knowledge did not put us at greater risk.

Picture now, a leather helmeted and goggled pilot wearing a bulky Mae West advancing to his aircraft, parachute strapped to his bottom with a holstered gun and belt, a machete eighteen inches long and with a six inch wide holstered blade, a survival kit strapped to his right leg, and a knife strapped at shoulder height and available to pierce his Mae West in the event of it automatically inflating in flight, with finally a rotund waist covering the thick belt with the gold coins.

Neither the Army nor the RAF had any knowledge or experience of tactical air support operations for front line troops in heavily jungled terrain. The Army was keen to have such support immediately preceding an advance and while the Japanese troops were recovering from the shock of the air attack. A plan was devised whereby immediately before our front line troops advanced they would fire verey lights into the air and we, the RAF troops would dive down and fly over their heads firing beyond the demarcation line indicated by the verey lights. On the first occasion we attempted this I was leading the four attacking Hurricanes, but had to abort the attack because as we started to dive down, the troops discontinued firing the lights and we could not accurately retain in our vision where precisely the demarcation line was; we had to ensure we did not hit our troops. On a second attempt the front line troops continued to fire the verey lights until we opened fire; this was successful but limited in use to those occasions when there existed a front line. But the concept of a front line soon became outdated in jungle warfare, being overtaken by the tactics of infiltration by small groups operating from fluid troop dispositions. On many occasions we were able to directly assist the Army by attacking enemy forward operating bases, which we could often identify, distributed among small jungle clearings. We developed a close liaison with the Army and it was rewarding planning together the forms of air support that were suitable and which existing service manuals and doctrines had not caught up with.

While on the subject of Army co-operation, on one occasion I had to lead a flight of six Hurricanes escorting the Commander-in-Chief, Field Marshall Wavell, south to the combat area. We took off, circled as his aircraft became airborne, and set off with my section in two way visual contact with his aircraft. I had briefed the other two sections to fly a few thousand feet above us in a position to sight any enemy fighters that might appear, and where they could warn me and if necessary descend to attack enemy fighters trying to get within range of the Field Marshall's aircraft. Some Jap fighters had appeared but one section of the top cover had turned towards them and they had withdrawn. The Field Marshall's aircraft had landed on a forward airstrip at Maungdaw and we returned to base. Later that day we flew south, rendezvoused with his aircraft and escorted it back to Chittagong without incident. After landing and feeling relieved that we had done a good job, I received a message that the Field Marshall wished to see me. I went up by

Jeep to the far side of the airfield to his tent/temporary HQ and was greeted by an officious major who informed me that the Field Marshall was angry because when the escort had taken off in the morning, the Hurricanes had blown off his hat and covered his party in dust. I thought, 'Bloody hell, is this the thanks we get.' I replied 'I'm sorry Sir' saluted and started back to my Jeep. At that moment a voice called out 'Pilot Officer Kitley' and the Field Marshall emerged from his tent. He thanked me for escorting himself and two American generals safely, told me not to worry about his hat and the major, and that it was his own fault for standing in a stupid place to watch the Hurricanes take off. Having decided a few moments beforehand that if given the chance I'd shoot his aircraft down next time, I thought what a gentleman he was and went off feeling good.

I think the most nerve-racking operations that we flew involved flying over the Chin Hills and penetrating into central Burma to attack either planned or opportunity targets. This type of operation was called a 'rhubarb', the name given to a similar type of operation flown from the UK involving flights of aircraft penetrating deep into central Europe. In our case they were normally flown by independent sections of two aircraft either by day or on moonlit nights. The targets were normally the lines of communication following the Irrawady River, - the railways, roads and the river itself. These operations were nerve-racking because the route across the Chin Hills meant climbing to 15,000 feet over heavily jungled and rocky terrain where engine failure meant curtains. When over the Hills you descended rapidly to ground level. If by night, you had the comfort of the unlikelihood of being intercepted by enemy fighters but at the same time the worry that you might fly into obstructions. If by day, you could clearly see the ground obstructions but you had to be wary of being intercepted. Once you had descended into Burma the Hills cut off any radio communication between you and base. You had the comfort of being able if necessary to talk to each other but radio silence to avoid detection was the order of the day, and prudent.

The targets on the 'rhubarbs' I flew were all in the Mandalay area. For those interested in the geography of Burma they were Chauk, Kyaukpadaung and Magwe. These targets were all some 250 miles away and even with our long-range tanks, time spent attacking the targets had to be limited to ensure sufficient fuel to fly the 250 miles back to base. On one of these 'rhubarbs' the two of us left twelve petrol goods wagons blazing with damage to the railway installations; on another we attacked riverboats. To witness at night a paddle steamer's engine room and boiler blow up as you pulled out of a dive was to say the least exhilarating. On a third occasion we blew up a train and wreaked havoc on some fifty freight cars. Because of our fuel state we normally did not stay around to note in detail the degree of destruction. The return journey was the trickiest part of the operation. We would now be out of ammunition, weaving like mad and flying as low as we could to avoid interception while realising that, if we had taken the Japs by surprise, they certainly now knew of our presence. Ahead of us was an hour's flying over hostile territory and the climb up to clear the Chin Hills. It was then that you listened intently to every little hiccough from the engine, scanned the temperature and the oil pressure gauges and kept your fingers crossed while hoping you still had sufficient fuel to get back. Having cleared the Hills a gradual descent to base came with a sigh of relief. On landing it was not unusual to find you had lost some 5lbs in weight and were soaked to the skin. These were dangerous missions. In roughly a span of two months we probably flew, in sections of two, about two dozen 'rhubarbs' but two pilots failed to return and many had lucky escapes, returning with evidence of having caressed the trees and broken the odd telephone line. In fact one of our pilots landed safely with thirty feet of electric cable wrapped around his wing. A tribute to the robust construction of the Hurricane.

    The flying over the Arakan was pretty intense and come the end of March 1943 our aircraft were beginning to have seen better days. Limited reserves of new Hurricanes were now being assembled in India. On 23rd March we flew combat missions in the morning and later flew, via Alipore, to an RAF Maintenance Unit at Allahabad, - five hours flying away. We returned the next day in new Hurricanes and were back in operations later that afternoon. The new Hurricanes were Mark 2cs, the difference being that they had twelve Browning machine guns mounted on their wings as against the eight guns we had in our Hurricane 2bs. The extra four guns made the Hurricane heavier and a little less manoeuvrable but the increased firepower was effective, particularly when attacking troops and other ground targets; firing at the rate of 7,200 rounds per minute the Hurricane 2c was a formidable adversary. Although Spitfires were still hoped for, it was then no more than a hope, but at least we had left behind the days when we were expected to fly aircraft with 'not fit for operational flying' stamped on their logbooks.

There were a number of incidents worthy of recall, - some of them pure Hollywood! On one Sunday morning we had six Hurricanes on 'readiness' at dawn. The RAF padre set up in our dispersal hut a small altar and communion rail. The ground crews joined us in the Service and just as the sacraments were being offered the order came through to 'scramble'. We rushed to the aircraft, roared off and at 20,000 feet received the order to 'pancake'; the Japs had turned back. On landing the padre welcomed us back and we continued with the Service, with the exception of some of the ground crews who had to refuel the aircraft and bring them back to a state of 'readiness'.

On another occasion, it was again dawn and we were sitting in our aircraft, oxygen turned fully on to counter the effects of hangovers; a not unusual action following the night before drinking bouts. A very senior officer who came visiting commended us on being alert and set to go before dawn had broken!

Another incident involved an inexperienced replacement pilot. On his first operational sortie he was scrambled in a formation of ten aircraft. There was a bit of a ding-dong with some Jap fighters and having returned to base we were debriefing and sorting out our possible claims; these would be in the categories of Jap aircraft 'destroyed', 'probably destroyed' or 'damaged'. The new pilot reported that he had fired at a bomber, thought he may have hit it but felt he could not claim it even as 'damaged'. Now it so happened that while he was relating his story the armourers were reporting that his guns had not been fired, and this was confirmed by the canvas fabric stuck over his gun portholes being intact. He was overcome with embarrassment, followed by tears, at having made a false statement. Some of us had sympathy with him. A raw inexperienced pilot on his first engagement with enemy aircraft would have felt apprehensive, insecure, even inadequate, but want to feel, and be seen as, a contributing member of the team. So, hearing the others giving vivid descriptions of their encounters he had been emotionally swept along and added his false bit. Fortunately his claimed involvement had been modest and innocuous and we agreed not to take the matter further. He subsequently developed into an effective fighter pilot.

This prompts me to refer to the sensitive subjects of 'bravery' and 'cowardice', - character traits which because of their personal nature we avoid discussing or ascribing to individuals. But there was a small minority of pilots who, while happy to risk the normal hazards of flying, were not happy to extend that risk to combat. But I repeat they were a small minority. Such pilots had may plausible reasons why they had broken off an engagement or not pressed home their attack. Aeroplanes can have a number of dysfunctions in the air which can justify a pilot returning to base; but these can cease to be apparent after landing. A spluttering or misfiring engine could have corrected itself after landing when revved up by ground crews; an oil pressure gauge could stick in the air and then work perfectly well after landing; sand dust in the petrol filter could have cleared when examined by the ground crews; a faulty magneto could excuse a pilot returning whereas those keen to continue might risk flying on one remaining magneto. High engine temperature coupled with the smell of burning rubber could be another justifiable cause of concern. Now each of these reasons can be genuine, but when they all tend to happen to one pilot and when the enemy is about, you start to worry. You worry because when flying together for mutual support you might be left isolated at the very time you need that support. I recall a particular pilot who on a number of occasions when things got hot reported his engine playing up, and returned to base. One or two of us exchanged experiences we had had with him, but although we felt that something should be done we recognised that the evidence was circumstantial. However it reached a stage when action had to be taken. On that occasion he was to accompany me on a 'rhubarb' into central Burma. I warned the authorising officer that when we climbed up to clear the Chin Hills he would report a defect in his engine and return to base, I also said that when that happened I would carry on on my own; this was against procedure but I had no intention of being tainted by his action and returning with him to base. Everything happened as forecast. When he transmitted to me that his aircraft was unserviceable and that we would have to return to base, I told him to get stuffed and carried on. However this incident brought things to a head and shortly afterwards he was quietly posted away from the squadron. It is also relevant to add that such pilots tended to be those who fortuitously would come across a single enemy aircraft when no other Hurricanes were around, and shoot it down. But oh dear what a pity - they would be over enemy territory so that their claim could not be verified or their falsehood exposed. The reputation of such pilots, and I must emphasise they were very few in number, soon spreads around and they would gradually become isolated, friendless and shunned by their peers.

I have given scant attention to the part played by our ground crews. Their tasks were to keep the aircraft serviceable but their effectiveness in doing that was very dependent on the concept of the 'team spirit'. Each Hurricane had a pilot, a fitter and a rigger. They could form a closely-knit team working together and in harmony if the chemistry was right; if the ground crew developed a respect for the pilot which could be matched by his respect for them, then the team gelled. A synergetic influence would evolve; aircraft would be refuelled and serviced in record time; the three might join together to clean the aircraft thus getting that little extra speed in flight; the fitter and rigger would rush to help the pilot out of the cockpit and be the first to want to know how the trip had gone; any success the pilot had would transfer across to them. If you were a good team then other tradesmen, such as armourers and wireless mechanics, who might have to attend to a number of aircraft, would give your team priority attention. This team spirit could be powerful and I have known ground crew members breakdown in tears when their pilot and aircraft failed to return from an operation.

The RAF had laid down that a fighter pilot's operational tour of duty would comprise of 200 operational flying hours. The term 'operational' roughly applied to hours flown when engaging the enemy or when being exposed to an enemy threat. Pilots would then be posted for a minimum of six months for a 'rest' before returning to operations. I was the first pilot on the squadron to reach 200 hours and in mid May 1943 I was posted as a flying instructor to an Operational Training Unit at Risalpur in the North West Frontier region of India. My brief was to convert newly trained pilots to Hurricanes and to instruct them in fighter tactics applicable to fighting the Japanese.

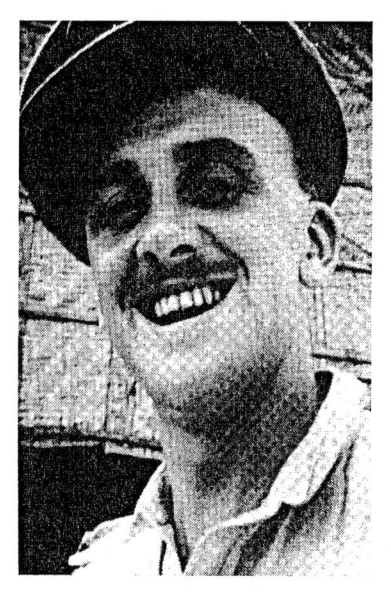

Kit off for a rest

Thus my approx. two years with 136 Squadron came to an end; little did I realise that before the war was ended I was to return as its squadron commander. But much was to happen before then.

CHAPTER SIX
IS THIS WHAT THEY CALL A 'REST'?

It was now mid May 1943 when I set off from Chittagong at the start of my journey to Risalpur. I flew by RAF Dakota to Calcutta and contacted the RAF Movements Branch regarding my onward journey. I had not experienced travel across India other than by air and was intrigued by the prospect of the three day journey by rail. As an officer I travelled first class and in an air-conditioned carriage with sleeping berth. Surprise was expressed by the other first class passengers that I was not attended by a personal 'bearer', - an Indian servant who would see to my needs. A British civil servant insisted that his bearer would look after me. I had no idea what 'looking after me' entailed, but it became apparent when at every stop he appeared with drinks and cool water to freshen up. Main meals were served at railway stations and the bearer would arrange a table, order and serve the meal; the length of stay at these stations depended on the time we took to eat the meal; the train left when we, the first class passengers were ready. This was just one example of the arrogance of the 'British Raj' and reflected the attitude generally of the majority of the British residents in India.

I was to find life and living conditions on the Frontier very different from those I had experienced in Bengal. While Bengal appeared over populated the Frontier region seemed to have much more space; living was cleaner, extreme poverty was less apparent. The Frontier Indians were predominantly Pathans; they were a proud race who seemed self-assured and confident; they accepted authority and discipline but only when exercised by those they respected. I believe they preferred being ruled by the British rather than come under the control of a 'non Moslem' independent Indian government. When independence came to India in 1947 under Mr Jinnah, they helped to form the independent state of Pakistan. The ensuing war between Pakistan and India was a blood bath and to this day relations between the two countries continue to be based on an uneasy peace, with at the time of writing, Kashmir being the bone of contention.

Risalpur was a garrison town. It was one of the bases for the Indian Army and Air Force engaged in their historical and still current role of suppressing inter tribal disputes and resisting encroachments from Afghanistan, the latter mainly through the infamous Khyber Pass. Being some 2,000 miles from Burma, the war had made little impact on the lifestyle of those serving in the NW Frontier. I was able to sample life as it had been and still was under the administration of the British Raj. The Officers' Mess was a most impressive and well appointed establishment; there was plenty of high quality food and drink, and to be served with bacon, steaks, roasts and fish along with a wide range of fruits and cheeses, was in stark contrast to the muscle bound goat meat which had been our staple diet in Burma. My quarter was a bungalow with lounge, bedroom, kitchen, bathroom and patio, - well furnished and equipped. I had to employ a staff consisting of a bearer who supervised the work of a water carrier, a guard, a gardener and a cleaner. I paid the wages of this staff of five, the total wage bill being some 60 rupees per month, - approx £5 in sterling. There was a routine, particularly in the Mess, that had to be followed. Each officer's bearer had to be in the dining room for every meal and standing at attention behind the officer's chair; he would serve the meal and drinks etc. and be available after dinner for any task the officer required. Every morning the bearer would bring tea and a small snack, draw my bath and lay out my newly cleaned and starched uniform; he would then go to the Mess to be ready when I arrived for breakfast. My sports clothes would also be laid out when required. In the evening my bath would be drawn and fresh clothes laid out. When I returned to the bungalow at night my bed would be turned back with dressing gown, pyjamas etc laid out. In my first few weeks I was in constant debt to the Indian tailors with all the clothes I had to have. I remember my bearer being most upset when I told him I did not need a dressing gown; he explained emotionally that he would not be able to hold his head high if 'his Sahib not having dressing gown'. I was now approaching my twenty first birthday and I revelled in all this newfound gracious living. The biggest discomfort was the heat. Temperatures went as high as 120F in the shade; the heat was so intense that we flew from 6.00am to

11.30am and when necessary restarted at 5pm when it was beginning to cool off.

Risalpur was a newly formed Operational Training Unit (OTU) similar to the OTU I had attended two years earlier at Usworth on my return from Canada and before joining 136 Squadron. Pilots arrived direct from flying training and had to convert to operational flying and operational aircraft, in this case the Hurricane. As instructors we had to teach them how to fly the dual controlled Harvard monoplane, clear them when ready to fly solo, then teach them operational manoeuvres before letting them loose on Hurricanes. The difference between the two OTUs was that in 1941 there had been an urgent need for pilots and this, coupled with limited training resources, had meant rushing our somewhat inadequate operational training. Now, whereas we had less than 100 hours flying when we were awarded our 'Wings', pilots arriving at Risalpur from training had some 200 hours, and because of improved resources were about to undertake a more thorough and rigorous operational training. Three or four pilots from the fighter squadrons in Burma had joined me at Risalpur, so together we were able to develop a training programme. Our only problem was that none of us was a trained flying instructor. We taught ourselves how to instruct and to cope with the tensions of being responsible for the trainee and aeroplane, while allowing the trainee freedom to learn and experiment with manoeuvres, which if not flown competently, could result in an accident. When to take over control is the problem facing flying instructors; if you take over control too early the trainee does not learn; if too late then - curtains!

First of all we had to instruct them on the Harvard and, when we considered they were ready, authorise them to fly solo. After a few hours solo we then started teaching the operational flying techniques. In the dual control Harvard we taught close and open formation flying, how to attack enemy aircraft from different attack directions, how close to get before opening fire, how to break off the attack, how to attack a ground target, angle of dives and speeds, how to fly very low to avoid ground fire, how to dog fight with enemy fighters, how to manoeuvre to get an enemy fighter off your tail and so on. Following this we put them into Hurricanes and led them through the various manoeuvres they had learnt in the Harvard.

And so this was life at Risalphur; up early and flying until 11.30am; drinks and lunch followed by a siesta; sports in the latter afternoon (if not flying); more gracious living in the evenings. But there are fools in all of us and after flying, and in the midday heat, a colleague and I would play squash before lunch. Little surprise then that the day came when I collapsed on the squash court and was rushed to hospital with a temperature of 108F. At the hospital I had blocks of ice laid on and around me and although it was touch and go, my temperature reduced rapidly and left me alive but with heat exhaustion; within 24 hours I had additionally developed pneumonia and jaundice, along with a stomach ulcer.

After four weeks in hospital I was given four weeks sick leave. I set off by train from Nowshera, a small town near to Risalpur, intending to go to Srinaga in Kashmir. On the way I stopped off at Murray, a hill station on the slopes of the Himalayas; there I bumped into four fellow pilots from Burma, two from 136 Squadron, who were on leave before taking up instructor posts at the OTU at Risalpur. We relived old times and talked about what they could expect at Risalpur. I never got to Srinaga; socialising in Murray helped my recuperation, apart from the ulcer. On return to Risalpur in mid September I was passed fit for flying. Although we now had four more instructors we were having to fly at maximum effort because of increased trainee intakes; in the remaining three weeks of September I flew 54 instructional sorties. I was informed that my six months 'rest' tour would finish at the end of the year when I would return to operational flying in Burma. Until the end of the year life continued without drama, apart from two weeks in November when I was back in hospital with dysentery!

Shortly after receiving orders that I would return to operational flying at the end of the year (1943), I was visited by a staff officer from Air Headquarters. He explained that the Prime Minister, Mr Churchill, had given instructions that the Indian Air Force was to be expanded, and that two squadrons in that expansion were to be fighter squadrons. The two squadrons were to be sent into Burma as soon as they could be deemed operational. It had been decided that while the personnel would be predominantly Indian, the key posts would be filled initially by RAF personnel; those RAF personnel would be withdrawn when it was deemed prudent to do so. The squadron and flight commanders along with four pilots would be experienced operational RAF pilots; the remaining twenty five pilots would be Indians. Similarly, RAF technical SNCOs along with some RAF technicians, would organise the aircraft servicing structure and help to train the Indian technicians before being withdrawn.

The squadron commander was to be a senior flight commander from one of the squadrons we had flown with in Burma; he was being promoted to squadron leader. The senior flight commander was also coming from one of the Burma squadrons, and I was to have accelerated promotion to flight lieutenant and become the second flight commander. I was obviously pleased about my promotion, as I had only been commissioned for two years. I was however thoughtful about the future; taking a newly formed squadron on operations with predominantly inexperienced personnel would be a challenge. That challenge became greater when orders came through that the squadron, No 9 Indian Air Force Squadron, was to form at Bhopal in mid January '43 and would be sent to Burma before the end of March. As some nark said, 'sling them into the deep end and those that survive should show promise.'

I left Risalpur at the end of December 1943. We had continued with flying training over Christmas, and it is interesting to note that we accepted the need for this without question. This 'press on' attitude tended to permeate all the British Forces and was, I believe, a significant influence on the ultimate British success in winning the war. Size of the Forces and equipment were obviously important, but the determination to win plugged any shortcomings that might have resulted in defeat when experienced by other cultures.

After an uneventful but wearying journey to Lahore I met with the other flight commander. Our squadron commander had recently crashed and was in hospital; it was to be some six weeks before he would be able to join us at Bhopal. That night the other flight commander and I got to know each other; we underwent what in modern parlance would be called a bonding experience; in fact as I recall, or cannot recall, we got drunk. The following day we met with the Air Officer Commanding (AOC) the RAF fighter group in Burma. He confirmed that he intended to send No 9 IAF Squadron into the forward operational area in March/April, and further confirmed that by early September Indian officers, SNCOs and airmen would take the place of all RAF personnel. The likely Indian squadron and flight commanders would in the meantime gain operational experience by being attached to the RAF squadrons operating in Burma.

I had felt from the start that from my experience at Risalpur, we would need at least eight RAF pilots rather than the four planned. However we decided that our case would be unlikely to be accepted until we could base such a recommendation on our experiences as we developed the squadron's operational ability. The AOC invited us out that evening and after more alcohol bonding wished us luck, adding with a wry grin, 'I think you'll need it!' Two Hurricanes had been positioned at the Lahore airfield and the following day we took off to fly to Bhopal via Delhi accompanied by debilitating hangovers.

Bhopal was the capital of the princely state of that name and the Maharajah's Palace was within a few miles of the airfield. He welcomed us and offered the squadron much hospitality, which included permission to go shooting on his land whenever we wished; I think the two of us went on some three hunting trips. The only incident of note was when a tiger appeared out of the undergrowth and growled; at the time I was standing in the Jeep with a .303 rifle at the ready hoping to sight some prey. My colleague at the wheel accelerated forward in some panic, I fell backwards over the tailboard on to the road, the rifle went off and fortunately we never saw the tiger again. I was to say the least grazed and bruised and, temporarily at least, lost my desire to go hunting.

The squadron personnel were already assembling at Bhopal under the control of a newly appointed RAF squadron adjutant. He was a recently commissioned ex warrant officer who had served in the RAF for some twenty years in the admin branch. He was to do a first rate job in helping to administer the squadron in the next eight months. Within two weeks of arriving the squadron complement was virtually complete with some 30 pilots, 25 SNCOs and approximately 300 other ranks. In addition we had a very large number of non-uniformed enrolled personnel, who carried out toilet and general cleaning duties and any other demeaning tasks. They were mainly the 'untouchables' along with others such as water carriers, char and dhobi wallahs, (launderers) etc. This type of task demarcation was our first experience of the complexities of managing an Indian squadron.

We drew up a training programme introducing them to flying in small to large formations, and carrying out exercises aimed at developing their ability to master all aspects of flying such as flying the Hurricane to its limits, advanced aerobatics, high speed dives, tail chasing and so on. The training load was heavy and in response to a request that we put to Air Headquarters in Delhi, three senior pilots recently arrived from the UK and who were awaiting posting to the Burma squadrons, were lent to us to help in the training. They were experienced fighter pilots and we were grateful for their assistance during the short time they were with us. We also had four more RAF pilots posted in to reinforce the experience we would need when we were moved into Burma. There were no facilities for live air firing exercises and we were pleased when told that before being sent on operations in Burma, the squadron would attend a three week air firing programme at a newly formed training school at Armarda Road, an airfield recently established in Bengal. This school specialised in all aspects of air firing and was staffed by some of the pilots who had been with me in Rangoon and Chittagong.

The squadron commander caught up with us in mid February having been medically passed fit for flying. In early March we received orders to move the squadron on or about the 23rd March, to Kalaura an airfield on the Assam/Burma border. We were to detach the aircraft, pilots and a nucleus of servicing personnel to Armarda Road for the three week air firing programme; then return to Kalaura by the 24th April when the squadron would be deemed 'operational' and required immediately to be available for operational flying against the Japanese.

By the end of February we were concerned as to whether the squadron would have attained operational standards by the 24th April. The flying standard was developing slowly and barely adequately. As I remember, we had had four crashes, two of which had been fatal, the other two resulting in severe injuries to the pilots. Three or four pilots were emerging as good embryo fighter pilots and developing leadership qualities in the air. But they were matched with those who lacked confidence in mastering the Hurricane; they could take off and land but caution was their watchword when it came to what they did in between. A number of those, mainly at their request, were to leave the squadron for more training in the next few months.

A further problem concerned the technical and servicing personnel. Many had been given a minimum of training and were having difficulties in mastering the servicing requirements of a Hurricane. I recall on one occasion approaching the airfield with a spluttering engine, which cut dead at 300 feet; I carried out a dead stick landing. The petrol filter was choked with sand and, when I took it out of its housing under the engine, the fitter looked at me as though I was a magician; he hadn't known it was there. Our RAF and the more experienced Indian servicing personnel were working hard to keep the aircraft flying while at the same time giving further instruction to those who needed it. Language aggravated the problem and limited effective communication.

But these were difficulties, which, though worrying, we could grasp and deal with. However, starting to emerge was a less tangible problem; one of low morale manifesting itself in a lack of cohesion, - a lack of team spirit. Normally one could say that such a situation indicated a lack of effective leadership by the squadron and flight commanders. But in this case we detected initially that there was a mounting tension between the Indian pilots, who individually were a mixture of Muslims, Sikhs, Parsees, Christians, Hindus and Anglo-Indians. When the squadron had formed in January they had not allowed differences in race, caste and culture to weaken their enthusiasm and resolve to co-operate to forge a cohesive unit, which would be a credit to the Indian Air Force and take its place in the defence of India. But over the weeks their differences had started to surface. The national situation did not help. Although the Indian leaders had the support of the majority of the Indian nation in demanding self-government and independence from the British, differences as to the form that independence would take had become the great issue. The Hindus, the majority, wanted a single state run by them; the Moslems were determined to go for partition and form a separate state of Pakistan. I do not want to dwell more on this except to say that those differences between factions were becoming differences between individuals and this was detracting from high morale. Similarly the problem had its repercussions within the other ranks. Thus a picture was emerging whereby we were in danger of taking to the forward area, a squadron of barely adequately trained flying and ground personnel who followed disparate ideologies and cultures, which could detrimentally limit the degree of cohesion and team spirit vital for operational success and achievement. We were certainly far from the ideal when effectiveness of the whole becomes greater than the sum of the individual parts. The latter is not a platitude but an essential condition for maximum achievement in any organisation.

In the latter half of March an advance party of ground personnel set off for Kalaura. The journey of some 1,500 miles was by train and where necessary river ferry. The main party of some 300 plus personnel followed shortly afterwards. The aircraft flew to Kalaura in one day, landing at Allahabad and Alipore en route. Apart from one small drama the total move went well. The drama concerned the main party's train journey; the train had pulled into a siding and the squadron cooks were preparing a meal. Everyone was initially waiting for tea; preparing tea for 300 plus personnel was in itself no mean task. A number of 'untouchables' got to the tea first and this made it undrinkable for all the Indian personnel. A fresh brew had to be prepared but the ensuing commotion presented a challenge for our Cockney adjutant; he met the challenge well, shouting out orders using a vocabulary he had learnt in the East End. This included telling a dubious Buddhist priest, who chose that moment to arrive to 'administer to his flock', to "flock off!".

Kalaura turned out to be a newly built airstrip, situated by a tea plantation and surrounded by light jungle, on the Burma/Assam border. It had a single runway, which, after being roughly levelled, had been laid with an iron mesh for its surface. Fortunately the Hurricane, with its robust undercarriage, was able to take the rough landings that we all tended to make. The iron mesh runway was narrow and just long enough for landings as long as touchdowns were made at the beginning of the runway. The combination of a hard bumpy surface and a narrow runway of limited length made landings, particularly in heavy rain and in a crosswind, difficult. The pilots generally coped well, although we were to suffer a few accidents but without serious injury to the pilot.

Airfield accommodation consisted of plenty of adequate bamboo huts and furniture, a petrol driven generator, and intermittent piped water of doubtful quality. Our initial task was to organise an airfield as well as operate a squadron. Services such as for example fire, medical, postal, sewage etc had to be organised with the specialist personnel we had on the squadron. On the larger established airfields such services were provided to support the squadrons, and having to get them established and operating immediately was a demanding task. However it was heartening to see everyone - airmen, NCOs and officers, all enthusiastically pitching in with many of the problems at Bhopal forgotten, or put aside, in the keenness to show that the Indian Air Force could do the job.

We flew all the aircraft to Armarda Road in early April. The training in the air firing school was good; while mainly for the inexperienced pilots, we all took advantage of testing and improving our firing skills. Air to air firing involves a tricky technique and is very difficult to master. The target is moving at speed and likely to be manoeuvring; the attacking aircraft is a moving gun platform and the pilot has to aim ahead and along the line of flight to allow for target movement. It may sound obvious but the bullets have to hit the target and not where the target was when the guns were fired; the gun sight has to track along the anticipated line of flight of the target and at the moment of firing the attacking aircraft has to be flown smoothly, with no jerkiness or side slip. So to sum up, the technique is to attack with an overtaking speed and to manoeuvre so as to move the aiming point along the projected line of flight of the target;

when in range, normally 200 yards, to fire and break off the attack before flying into the target. That 200 yards is covered in no time when the attacking aircraft has for example a 100 mph overtaking speed. Attacking static or slow moving ground targets is less tricky unless, having got sights on and firing, the pilots get a bit mesmerised by the target, do not pull away in time, and fly into the ground, or fly into obstacles such as power cables also with fatal results.

The war situation had changed significantly since I had left the Burma area in June 1943. The Americans were now on the offensive and achieving successes in the Pacific. The initiative in the Mediterranean/North Africa regions had passed from the Germans to the Allies; Sicily and most of Italy were now in the hands of the Allies and the Italians had given up the struggle. Preparations were being made to launch the second front into Europe. The situation vis-a-vis the Far East and India was still critical. In spite of continuous and intensive fighting the position in the Arakan had changed little; the island of Akyab was still in Japanese hands and frustrating any advance by the Army further south towards Rangoon. The Japanese Army and Air Force had been reinforced and were now consolidated in Burma having reached the Indian border. They were threatening strategic places such as Kohima and Imphal to pave the way for a major offensive to invade India. But becoming more than an irritation to the Japanese were the Chindits long range penetration group under General Wingate; they had established a base in enemy occupied central Burma, built an airfield, 'Broadway' and by air supply were building up significant forces to launch an offensive behind Japanese lines. At the same time reinforcements were beginning to arrive from Europe and the Middle East and in particular Spitfires. The first squadron to get Spitfires was my old squadron, No 136, and on New Year's Eve 1943 the combination of experienced pilots and Spitfires resulted in the squadron destroying a formation of Japanese bombers and fighters over the Arakan with no loss to themselves. The Japanese Zeros were proving no match for the Spitfires flown by the RAF. This then was the situation when we returned to Kalaura on the 24th April. The combination of the training at Bhopal, rounded off by the intensive air firing training, had given the pilots new confidence and their morale was high in anticipation of operational flying. That morale was strengthened when the Air Commander in Chief, South East Asia Command (Air C in CSEA) sent a signal to say that No 9 IAF Squadron was now operational.

At this time Imphal and Kohima were under severe attack with the Japanese Army intent on breaking through to India. The Dakota squadrons were flying at maximum effort in delivering supplies and reinforcements. Our immediate task was to patrol the supply routes to protect the Dakotas from attack by Japanese fighters. Our patrol height was 14,000 feet with Spitfires covering us at 22,000 feet. But the Japanese fighters showed a reluctance to attack the Dakotas with Hurricanes in close proximity, and more particularly Spitfires ready to pounce. We had a few skirmishes with the Jap fighters but in the main they were chased off by the Spitfires before developing attacks on the Dakotas.

Good use being made of water tap

However in the first two weeks that the squadron operated from Kalaura, weather was becoming a greater threat than the Japanese fighters. Our patrols were over hilly terrain rising to 12,000 feet; the combination of the oncoming monsoons, coupled with the rising hot and moist air over the hills, heralded the build up of the giant cumulo nimbus cloud formations. Flying on instruments in cloud without a visual frame of reference requires experience and concentration; but, when the buffeting from the up currents within the cumulus nimbus clouds causes the instruments to behave erratically, an inexperienced pilot can be misled by false sensations concerning the behaviour and attitude of the aircraft and can quickly find his aircraft has gone out of control. His chances of regaining control relies on the height of his aircraft when it emerges from the cloud. His visual frame of reference is restored but he might need over 5,000 feet of ground clearance to regain control. The squadron suffered two fatalities in that two week period because of bad weather and a third pilot broke his leg after baling out.

STILL GOING STRONG: Hawker Hurricanes operated on the Burma front by the Indian Air Force

The monsoon broke on 11th May. We had spent most of the day maintaining a continuous cover of four Hurricanes defending Vengeance dive-bombers, which were attacking targets out of Imphal, and in between times, escorting Dakotas. There had been further skirmishes with the Japanese Zero fighters and the weather was quite appalling. I had temporarily grounded three pilots in my flight as they had recently joined the squadron and were not sufficiently experienced for flying in such weather, let alone coping with enemy fighters. I recall landing back at Kalaura late afternoon having flown 5.5 hours that day. We were two sections of four Hurricanes; the pilots were weary as we landed in heavy rain, gusting winds of gale dimensions, poor visibility and on the narrow flooded runway. One aircraft crashed but the pilot was uninjured although a bit 'shook up'. Orders had come through that the squadron was to abandon Kalaura and fly to a more permanent base at Khumbirgram some fifty miles away. The other Hurricanes had already left and I was to take this last flight of four Hurricanes to Khumbirgram after refuelling and rearming. I decided conditions were such that, coupled with the onset of night, we would delay until the following morning. I vaguely recall a heated field telephone conversation with a staff officer at Group Headquarters, who felt that pilot fatigue, bad weather, poor visibility in heavy rain, were poor excuses for not leaving that night. When I realised that he was not joking I told him when and where he could go. The following dawn we left a miserable looking and flooded Kalaura; what a joy to land at Khumbirgram in a weather lull and on a solid wide runway with plenty of length and in good visibility.

Khumbirgram was a semi permanent base for Vengeance dive-bombers with good airfield facilities and accommodation, but it was overcrowded. The Vengeance crews had guts; they flew a heavy, underpowered single engine aircraft, which, with a full bomb load, wallowed along and were sitting ducks to the Japanese fighters. At Khumbirgram we continued with the same type of operations that we had flown from Kalaura; these were patrolling the routes being flown by the Vengeance aircraft and in particular giving close escort to the air supply Dakotas. During the two weeks we operated from Khumbirgram the squadron lost, as I remember, two Hurricanes and one pilot, but was justifiably proud that no losses through enemy fighters, were recorded by either the Vengeance or Dakota aircraft, while having protection from our Hurricanes.

Towards the end of May we learnt that Kalaura had been put completely out of action by the monsoons and that our new base was to be Comilla some 300 miles to the south. On 28th May we said farewell to our hospitable hosts at Khumbirgram, and after an abortive attempt caused by bad weather finally landed at Comilla.

During our stay at Kalaura there had been a number of incidents that had added to the colour of our lives! I, along with five others, had shared a bamboo hut for our sleeping quarters. When a replacement pilot or visitor moved in with us we would recount our fictional stories concerning snakes. Then late that night and with the aid of a length of thread tied to a rope, a snake would be seen in the near darkness slithering across the floor. The newcomer was then likely to leap out of bed and out of the hut accompanied by our guffaws. However, in a sense the laugh was on us because, one evening the hut caught fire and as we watched helplessly the whole hut went up in flames. To our amazement we then witnessed over 100 cobras of varying sizes scuttle out of the roof and set off into the undergrowth; we had never before seen snakes on or around that hut!

On another occasion an Indian refuelling mechanic had to be reprimanded because he had not securely fixed the filler caps on the long range tanks of one of the Hurricanes; the caps had vibrated off in flight, petrol had leaked out, and the fire hazard was a real one. He was young, keen but with little mechanical experience. He went to the workshop and made a tightener bar some two feet long; with this extra leverage he was able to make sure that the caps screwed on tightly. Our problem then was that the heat from the excessive tightening had welded the caps onto the tank openings and half a dozen long-range tanks had to be replaced.

It seems that when things were going pretty well, a drama was waiting to happen. In the Officers' Mess dinner was being enjoyed - tough goat stew but who cares when hungry. Suddenly one of our Sikh pilots leapt to his feet in protest at having extracted from his mouth a piece of corned beef. All hell broke loose because in addition to the Sikhs the Hindus did not eat beef. When it all settled down the cooks promised not to allow such a lapse to occur again. This was accepted by the Sikhs and Hindus and I went back to my cold goat stew!

I had a central involvement in these and other dramas because during this period the squadron commander, for reasons I cannot recall, had been temporarily detached from the squadron and my brother flight commander had broken a leg on baling out and was in hospital. Thus I was officially in command and responsible for the efficient operation of the squadron, both in the air and on the ground.

We suffered casualties and the squadron was responsible for funeral arrangements. When operating from a permanent or large RAF Station, station support staff took over and made the appropriate arrangements for the funerals. We did not have that luxury. Furthermore in the RAF we were virtually all of the Christian faith with only small variations in the funeral services of the various denominations. Large bases also had padres on tap. Our, or my problem, was having to deal with the completely different religions and to ensure that due respect was paid to the sensitivities of each faith. Indian padres and priests were in theory available to help and officiate but in the jungle not readily available. I became very dependent on advice from the lay Indian personnel, who seemed well informed about the detailed funeral procedures that applied to their particular faith.

My first learning experience was having to arrange a funeral for one of our Hindu pilots. A Hindu padre was not immediately available and in the heat, time was of the essence in body disposal. With the help of the Sikh doctor I selected a suitable clearing in the jungle, and a working party of Hindu airmen volunteered to build the funeral pyre. I then, as chief mourner, joined a funeral party which carried the body of the deceased on a form of stretcher; the body was placed on the pyre and as I recall I had to put the flame to it. After 2/3 days and when the body was consumed I, as chief mourner, picked over the ashes, which were laid in a small urn and sent back to India with an officer for further funeral rites with the family. A Parsee pilot was killed and his body had to be escorted to Calcutta, where the special funeral rites involved it being exposed to the elements on a 'Tower of Silence' until it had completely decomposed. Bodies of Moslem pilots were sent, also under escort, to India for burial in a Moslem cemetery.

Our new base at Comilla was a semi-permanent airfield with a long, metallic runway. It was the base for part of the Dakota

Air Supply Force. Whereas we had assumed that we were to operate from Comilla because Kalaura was out of action and Khumbirgram over-crowded, it turned out that we had been moved south to strengthen the Arakan forces. For it transpired that, because of the continuing success of the army to frustrate the Japanese advance into India in the Imphal/Kohima area, the Japanese were strengthening their forces in South West Burma, to attempt a breakthrough into India from the Arakan and across the Chin Hills.

In the first part of June 1944 after arriving in Comilla, the squadron flying was intensive. In addition to escort and patrol duties we flew missions attacking targets in the Southern Arakan/Akyab Island areas. These included 'night rhubarbs'. 'Night rhubarbs' were hazardous missions because of the combination of range, the weather, anti-aircraft fire, navigation and difficulty of attacking targets while avoiding ground obstacles. The policy was to fly 'rhubarbs' when there was a half to full moon; but a full moon is of limited help in identifying targets and obstacles when it is obliterated by thick cloud and in heavy rain. The squadron commander and the other flight commander had by now rejoined the squadron. The three of us agreed that, because of the general conditions and the pilots' lack of night flying experience, the Indians should not fly any of the eight 'rhubarbs' being planned over the period 5 - 8 June. We decided they would be flown by the three of us along with two senior RAF pilots; in the event the conditions justified this decision. On one of the two 'rhubarbs' I flew in that period my log book records, 'Akyab island - attacked aircraft on ground and two large sampans, - anti-aircraft fire, weather terrible.' On landing my Hurricane was found to have suffered damage. On the other 'rhubarb' my log reads, 'Akyab, - attacked and blew up large paddle steamer, - slight anti-aircraft fire, weather lousy.' As we were getting near to the time when the squadron would become 'Indianised' we, on orders from Group HQ, organised night flying practices which had to be flown in addition to the day operations. Two Indian pilots were selected from my flight to fly two 'rhubarbs' on 24th June. The targets were in the southern Arakan at maximum range and the weather was poor. However our Group Headquarters insisted that Indian pilots were to be used; it was hinted that we were molly coddling them. I briefed them carefully: to return to base if weather bad; to descend through cloud only if sure of position; to divert on the way back to other airfields if short of fuel; and so on. They took off that night; one was never heard of again; the other sensibly returned after 2.5 hours having found the weather unsuitable in the target area.

We had an excellent Sikh doctor on the squadron; he had twice warned me in June that I was overdoing it and could be heading for exhaustion. Like any young man of twenty two years my reaction was to say 'Balls' and perhaps even to increase my workload and flying hours to demonstrate my fitness. However on reflection I now believe that having responsibility for the squadron during much of the time at Kalaura and when we were flying flat out on operations, probably had a debilitating effect on me. In a three week period I had flown fifty operational hours and on landing been involved with sorting out problems of food, funerals, aircraft serviceability, accident investigations, etc. etc. This probably helps to explain why I went down with a severe attack of pleurisy, which saw me four weeks in hospital followed by four weeks in a sanatorium in the hills.

It was towards the end of August before I rejoined the squadron and three weeks before Indian Air Force (IAF) personnel would replace the remaining RAF personnel. Some of the RAF pilots were having to stay on as, due to casualties, the squadron was under strength with IAF pilots. Indian newsreel cameras were sent to publicise the handover but little did they realise that the various formations we flew for their cameras involved more RAF than IAF pilots. The squadron had suffered casualties and insufficient numbers of replacement pilots had been available; so RAF pilot replacements had unbalanced the IAF/RAF comparative pilot strengths. However more replacement Indian pilots were now beginning to arrive, some of whom had been on the Armarda Road air-firing course. It had also been agreed that operational commitments would be temporarily reduced to allow for training hours to be flown.

On the subject of casualties and accidents, all squadron commanders had been sent a letter from the Air C in C, SEA concerning accidents. It included statistics, which showed that the accident rate of the RAF in SE Asia compared unfavourably with that of the Metropolitan Air Force (MAF) in the UK. The MAF were experiencing sixteen accidents per 10,000 flying hours, whereas in SE Asia we were having thirty six accidents per 10,000 hours. Further it appeared that we were destroying more of our own aircraft in accidents than the total of enemy aircraft we were destroying in combat. This letter and its statistics triggered off much controversy and a certain amount of resentment. They were statistics that could be open to misleading interpretation and, coupled with the tone of the letter, implied that our comparatively poor accident record was as a result of carelessness and inadequate leadership. No recognition was given to the comparative inexperience of our pilots vis-a-vis those in the UK; and the ramifications of our having had to fly for much of the war to date, second hand aircraft suitable more for the knackers yard rather than fighting the Japanese were not considered. Also weather was not referred to as a contributory cause of accidents; it was my belief that at times weather was our number one enemy, - awesome weather that could present difficulties for even experienced pilots when flying on instruments in highly turbulent clouds, with up currents that could take over the aircraft and put it out of control. Comparisons should not be made based on statistics when the premises and source material on which they are based is subject to different and varying operating conditions.

An accident that I will always remember because of the impact it made on me, concerned a Dakota air supply aircraft. We were to provide an escort of six Hurricanes for eight Dakotas taking supplies to the combat area in the Arakan. The Dakotas were also based at Comilla. As the last Dakota set off down the runway I, with my number 2, lined up on the runway and watched as it accelerated ahead of me. I then witnessed the most horrific accident imaginable. The Dakota had a cargo of drums of petrol; these must have broken loose and rolled to the back of the aircraft. As the Dakota became airborne the tail dropped and the nose rose; it climbed vertically to about 150 feet and hung in the air before falling on its back to one side of the runway where it exploded in flames. The sight of two figures emerging from the plane consumed in flames and running in all directions until they each collapsed dead, is one I will never forget. The crashed aircraft was close to, and clear of the runway, but scattered burning debris made it too dangerous to take off. I ordered engines to be switched off to avoid overheating and radioed the Dakota leader and suggested they set course for the target and we would catch up with them before entering enemy air space. I then noticed one of the Hurricane pilots had got out of his aircraft, removed his helmet and was walking off. I left my cockpit, went across to him and asked what he thought he was doing. He said he could not take off again after witnessing such an accident. I then thought I could either order him to return to his aircraft or give him a rational reason as to why he should return. I chose the latter and pointed out to him that we now had seven Dakotas who needed our protection. He wiped his eyes, apologised and climbed back into his cockpit. Within ten minutes the burning debris and bodies had been cleared off the runway and we took off and caught up with the Dakotas some thirty minutes later. It was as well we did, as Japanese fighters appeared and as we turned in towards them they turned and disappeared into a cloud. In flying at high speed to catch up with the Dakotas we had used more fuel than expected and on the return journey we had to land at Chittagong to refuel. We were then faced with another drama, more irritating than serious. Chittagong by then was a temporary base for an American squadron of Lightening twin boom fighters. USAF rations were more attractive than those of the RAF, whose officers had strict instructions not to eat any USAF food which might be laid out on tables in the Mess. In ignorance of this order we were putting peanut butter on our bread when challenged by a USAF officer who said he was reporting this sin to the RAF station commander. For the second time that day I suppressed my mouth from articulating my thoughts and at a sign from me the six of us rose, left the Mess, climbed into our refuelled Hurricanes and returned to Comilla. On the few occasions I eat peanut butter I always recall this incident. Needless to say our relations with the USAF were generally very good but one stupid member of a group can sour the image we retain of the group itself.

    Having spent some time in the past year in a field hospital, I must pay recognition to the professional and sympathetic treatment I was given. The RAF Princess Mary Nursing Service, coupled with the RAF doctors, certainly knew how to organise and operate a hospital under far from ideal conditions. What impressed me was that in spite of temporary housing in bamboo huts, tents, rain, mud and creepy crawlies, the Nursing Sisters were able to appear every day in immaculately laundered and pressed white uniforms. In the throes of a fever they looked and filled the role of ministering angels. I recall an anecdote concerning the Matron. A pilot had suffered injury in a crash, which included a bruised and lacerated 'willie'. A very attractive sister would come and bandage it, but shortly afterwards the bandage would come loose and fall off. The Matron appeared, ticked him off and told him that he must control himself. He was a brave man when he suggested to the Matron that it would probably stay on better if she were to bandage it!

Anticipating that in September the RAF personnel would be replaced, I had applied to return to operational flying and to take up a flight commander's appointment in a RAF Squadron, preferably flying Spitfires and hopefully in No 136 Squadron. I was told that I would have to await a vacancy and that it would be a long shot if such a vacancy happened to become available in No 136 Squadron. In the meantime I was to take up the appointment of flight commander at a Refresher Flying Unit that had been established in Poona.

Before setting off for Poona I must acknowledge how well the Indians developed and performed their various roles on the squadron. They had an enthusiasm which occasionally found them running before they could walk and with fatal results. But with the combination of enthusiasm, bravery and commitment many had matured into good fighter pilots and leaders.

CHAPTER SEVEN

PUNTING IN POONA

I found Poona to be a pleasant town situated some one hundred miles inland from Bombay. I believe it had its roots in the 18th century mainly as a garrison town for the East India Company security forces, later to become the basis of the Indian Army; it had also served as a sort of retreat for the British from the hustle and bustle of life in Bombay. Poona had developed the facilities typical of life in the Colonies; in this case a well-established club with full sporting, recreational and social activities and additionally a yacht club. Membership of such clubs was through application and selection by a committee and normally only available to British officials and British officers of the three Services. Indians, regardless of position and rank, and also others from non-white cultures, were not eligible for membership. Indeed, officers such as myself who were from working/lower middle class families, and the product of the state schools, were regarded with apprehension as not having the appropriate background and upbringing to equip them to participate fully and with confidence in the social routine of living within the structured hierarchy of the 'British Raj'.

It was now October 1944 and generally the war was going well. The Germans were on the defensive and retreating on all fronts. The Japanese were taking a battering from the Americans in the Pacific and being ejected by force, and with American guts, from the many islands they had invaded in their 1941/42 offensive. The fight for Burma was still intensive and with high casualties, but there was optimism that the now British 14th Army would make a breakthrough, overrun the over-stretched Japanese Army, and recapture Burma before advancing into Siam and down the Malay Peninsular to Singapore.

In the early stages of the war, a number of far seeing politicians and senior RAF officers had recognised that air power would play a vital role in achieving success. Facilities for training the likely numbers of aircrew required, were not available in the

United Kingdom. Thus the Empire Air Training Scheme (EATS) had come into being. Countries within the British Empire such as Canada, Australia, New Zealand, South Africa and Rhodesia agreed to develop, with RAF assistance, training facilities for pilots, navigators, air gunners and wireless operators. RAF trainees were sent overseas for such training and their numbers were bolstered by trainees needed for the expansion of the Dominion air forces, such as the Royal Australian Air Force (RAAF), Royal Canadian Air Force (RCAF), and so on. In the early days the Dominion trained aircrew joined RAF squadrons, but as the war developed the Dominion Air Forces expanded and formed their own squadrons. My training in Moosejaw was under the EATS and to demonstrate the value of the Scheme, when 136 Squadron formed at Kirton-in-Lindsey we had, in addition to those of the RAF, pilots from the Dominion Air Forces and from friendly countries who enrolled in the RAF. The success of this training organisation had provided the aircrew needed, but come 1944, with the enemy on the defensive, the need for rapid pilot replacement and pilots for newly formed squadrons was tailing off; casualty replacements and relief pilots were still needed but not in the numbers required in the 1940 - 44 years. So newly trained pilots were now arriving in India not having flown for some three months; they needed refresher flying and tactical flying experience. Thus there was a similarity between the roles of the OTU at Risalpur and the RFU at Poona.

      The fighter training squadron at Poona had two flights - one of Hurricanes and the other Spitfires; Harvard aircraft were additionally in both flights for dual instruction. I was in charge of the Hurricane flight. Up until Poona I had spent the past three years on operational and training flying duties; I had also had flight commander responsibilities. Although the training at Poona was to be quite intensive, I had sufficient instructors plus a deputy to lighten the load. So I resolved, as events allowed, to enjoy a period of relaxation coupled with sporting and social activities. I tried to limit my flying to instructing those who had difficulty in mastering some of the more demanding operational flying techniques. I also remained determined to pressurise Group Headquarters into giving me a flight commander post in an operational squadron, preferably in No 136 Squadron.

I settled into a pleasant routine at Poona; one or two flights in the morning and when needed, some night flying. In the four months at Poona I flew fifty day and twelve night hours, averaging fifteen hours per month; a significant reduction from the thirty hours per month I had until then averaged. I spent the first two months sailing virtually every afternoon reaching a reasonable standard. I was also able to maintain a regular intake of alcohol. Our Officers' Mess was a large commandeered house and some ten of us shared a bedroom; food was adequate but goat is unexciting and when we could afford it we ate out at a fashionable but expensive restaurant in the town.

Some three weeks before Christmas the Governor of Bombay sent an invitation for six officers to attend his ball at Government House, Bombay. With a week to go no volunteers had put their names down, and our station commander asked me to make up a party of six, arrange transport and make sure everyone behaved. So six reluctant volunteers set off in a 15cwt truck, shook hands with the Governor and his lady and made straight for the bar. We were delighted to find it well stocked and free. After an hour or so the Governor's ADC approached us saying 'I say you chaps, you're not playing the game, there are young ladies wanting to dance but have no partners, I beg you to join them.' We waited for the next dance to start and I led the reluctant part drunken five of them onto the dance floor for a 'Paul Jones'. I found myself dancing with a pleasant partner and as we separated I asked her if we could have the last waltz together. She said she had already agreed to have it with an army captain. My ungentlemanly reply was to say something like 'Please yourself' and return to the bar. But as the evening progressed I dwelt on this, sought her out, apologised and invited her to come to a Christmas party at our Mess in Poona a few days later; she accepted. As we left I noticed that she was not dancing; she came across, told me she had passed her army captain over to a friend and so we enjoyed the last waltz together. This was the start of a close 45-year relationship, which strengthened in the face of the many difficulties we were to meet.

Denise was tall, attractive and some seven years older than myself. Early on in the war she had been approached by the Special Forces Executive and asked to consider becoming involved with helping to organise the collaboration with the French resistance movement. Because of family connections she had been educated in France and attended the Sorbonne. She was fluent in the language and this, plus her knowledge of France and its culture, were the reasons why the intelligence forces had sought her out. So she joined a Unit called Force 135. They planned to train her as an agent. She was trained in armed and unarmed combat and was about to start parachute training, when it was decided that with her background she would be more useful working in the administration of the Unit. She became responsible for selecting agents, indoctrinating them into their role, and briefing them before being sent into France. She also liaised with industry in the development of small gadgets to help agents, such as disguised flick knives, small calibre guns disguised as fountain pens; additionally she was responsible for safeguarding the cyanide tablets for agents, who if caught, preferred that way out rather than be subjected to the hideous alternative of Gestapo torture.

Denise

After D-day the need for Force 135 became less critical. Denise was asked to go with a small experienced group to India to set up a similar organisation for infiltrating agents into Japanese occupied territory. It was suggested that for personal safety reasons she went into uniform as an officer in the First Aid Nursing Yeomanry (FANY). She declined this offer preferring to stay a civilian; also, as she told me, she was not enamoured with the prospect of being referred to as a FANY!

The new Unit was titled Force 136 and at that time had its centre at Kirkee some ten miles from the airfield at Poona. Because of the heat they worked long mornings and so we were able to meet up most afternoons. Our transport was bicycles and our favourite leisure activity was spending most nights in a punt on a river near Kirkee. We would part at 5am; I would cycle like mad the ten miles to the airfield and by 7am would be in the air giving flying instructions. How wonderful to be young! On a couple of weekends we went by train to a small resort fifty miles from Poona, stayed at a rather grotty hotel with indifferent food, but enjoyed every minute of it. After Christmas we spent a week at a first class hotel at Aurangabad in Hyerabad state. This was some 200 miles from Poona and I was able to persuade the RAF to fly us there and back in an Anson aircraft.

Towards the end of January my posting back to operations came through. I could hardly believe my luck; I was to join 136 Squadron at Minneriya in Ceylon as the senior flight commander. Having got what I wanted, I realised that I no longer had the freedom of independence that I had enjoyed since leaving for India in 1941. I was concerned about the effect this could have on my relationship with Denise. She had a similarly independent spirit and I wondered how we would manage this turn of events. Do we accept the uncomplicated simplicity of a parting, giving lip service to thoughts of meeting some time in the future; or do we face the complications that would arise if we put our relationship as a No 1 priority and on a formal footing? Neither of us had discussed what was meant by our relationship. Was it a brief encounter, such as I had had with Gladys Chamberlain in Hampton Wick when I was twelve years old? Was it a 'here today, gone tomorrow' relationship, as I had had with Madge the barmaid in Kirton-in-Lindsay in 1941; or was it emotionally deeper and bordering on some sort of permanence? I found the thought of the latter with its complexities more worrying than my first flight in a Hurricane. I need not have worried. Denise was pleased I had got the posting I had wanted; as she said, she had heard little more since we had met about my going back on operations and preferably to 136 Squadron and had accepted that this might happen. Anyway as she said, our wartime careers would inevitably mean separation. She did however make the point that whatever the future it would help if I didn't get myself killed. With that I had no argument! After a couple of days I phoned her and suggested we get married. Her reaction was to ask if I was making a proposal and if so she accepted, and pointed out that had I asked her two days earlier she would have had nine rather than seven days to organise a wedding.

There was no arguing about the wedding arrangements. I was for a registry office with a couple of beers; she insisted on a white wedding, bridesmaids, full church service with organ and choir, a reception at the RAF Officers' Mess and a honeymoon in the hotel we stayed in on leave in Aurangabad. While Denise took over the wedding arrangements I, under pressure, bought a sports jacket for the honeymoon and then applied myself to flying a Spitfire. 136 Squadron was now equipped with Spitfire VIIIs, - the latest mark of Spitfire. Virtually all my flying experience had been on Hurricanes, - a fast highly manoeuvrable aeroplane, robustly constructed, and as such a pilot's friend. I loved that aeroplane and regretted that I had never quite achieved 1000 hours flying in the Hurricane. It had saved my life on many occasions and withstood enemy fire and damage that would have destroyed most aeroplanes. But now, the Spitfire; elegant and sleek in appearance with razor edged wings and a souped up Merlin engine that needed a four bladed propeller to absorb its power. Sitting in the cockpit was akin to fitting on a glove; the cockpit design gave the pilot easy access to the various controls and instruments. Its attributes also included full air conditioning, automatic oxygen feed, and to counter any suggestions that it was beautiful rather than practical, it had the firepower of four Browning machine guns and 2 x 20 millimetre canons. Its speed and acceleration were breathtaking, and like any lady she needed careful and thoughtful consideration but with firm handling. On take off the gyroscopic effect of the large four bladed propeller on full power could cause the Spitfire to rear 90° off the runway and crash; this could only be corrected by the pilot applying full rudder bias, and having the strength in the left leg to maintain this bias if the Spitfire was to keep straight on the runway. On landing she could be a bitch; unless you put her down gently she could rear up and put on a display of petulance by kangarooing down the runway, bending the undercarriage and damaging the tips of the propeller blades.

Events now started to move quickly. Weddings cost money. Denise's mother had died some time before Christmas and she had been left a small inheritance. She telegraphed for the money to be transferred to her in India; I paid for the sports jacket! We met with the vicar, a little tubby man called Canon Ball who was amusingly delightful as his title and name. The ceremony went off well and without a hitch apart from the taxi running out of petrol when taking the bride to the church; also from the church to the reception the same taxi had a puncture, but as there was only half a mile to go we bumped along regardless. After the reception we went by RAF car to the airfield; the Anson was beribboned and with old boots tied to the tail wheel and we took off with our friends cheering and waving.

The hotel at Aurangabad welcomed us with a very pleasant champagne reception. With all the excitement of the past week Denise was feeling a little tired and under the weather, and retired to her bed. Before her bed became our bed she had developed a high temperature and was carried off by ambulance to a British army hospital where severe jaundice was diagnosed. There were other medical complications and for two days her condition was critical. Having survived the crisis period, it then became apparent that she would be in hospital for some time. I arranged for a Harvard to fly me back to Poona, where I got an assurance from the RAF that when she was fit to be moved they would arrange an airlift to the army hospital in Poona.

Married 8 February 1945 at St. Mary's Church, Poona

Leaving for honeymoon

I then set off for Bombay from where I flew by Dakota to Colombo, Ceylon, via Madras. From Colombo I cadged a ride in a Vengeance dive-bomber to Minneriya where I expected to find 136 Squadron. The Squadron was there but grounded with the Spitfires being dismantled and put in crates. All personnel were under strict security orders not to discuss the situation with anyone. Rumours abounded. The squadron was obviously on the move but to where? 'Where' was likely to be well beyond the range of the Spitfires otherwise why crate them up? After a few days I received news from Poona that Denise had been moved to the hospital in Poona; she was progressing well but slowly. I could not contact her because security precautions forbade any contact with those not involved in whatever operation the squadron was likely to be engaged.

Duck shooting around many of the lakes in Ceylon became our only relief from boredom. It was now mid March 1945 and orders came through that we were to embark by ship to a secret destination. We were given printed letters to send to relatives and friends in the UK. These in essence said that it might be some time before they received further correspondence, that the sender was well and there was no need to worry! The only addition we could make to the letter was to write the name of the addressee and to sign it for example 'love, Alan.' Though well intentioned I believe the letter created more concern to the receiver than the comfort it hoped to give.

As soon as we had embarked and the convoy was underway we were briefed on our destination and the purpose of the operation. The Allied grip was tightening on Japan. American forces had regained most of the islands in the Pacific, including the Philippines. They were now preparing for an invasion of the Japanese homeland starting with Honshu, one of the four main islands of Japan and to the south west of Honshu, the capital island at the heart of the Japanese empire. At the same time the British were preparing for an onslaught on Singapore, the centre of power and influence over the Japanese occupied territories in the vast area of South East Asia. If Singapore fell it would only be a matter of time before the whole of South East Asia was recovered.

Our destination was to be the Cocos and Keeling islands. These were situated in the Indian Ocean some 3,000 miles to the south east of Ceylon and some 2,000 miles from the nearest point in Australia. The nearest land mass was Sumatra some 800 miles away. We were part of an 'invasion' force although it was anticipated that the small indigenous population would be friendly. The plan was to take over the islands and build an air base from which a large force of RAF Liberator bombers would launch attacks on Singapore and other key targets. The role of 136 Squadron was to defend the islands from aerial assault. It was believed that once the Japanese knew of the existence of the base and its massive bomber force it would be a priority target for their navy; and although the Japanese navy had taken a beating from the Americans they still had aircraft carriers, one of which could be deployed to neutralise the base.

The Cocos were islands of coral grown and built up from the undersea rim of a defunct volcano. This would have resulted, in theory, in a circular island surrounding a lagoon. However because of the variable coral growth the circle was fragmented and comprised a number of small islands. The largest island, Home Island, was where the natives lived; all the other islands were uninhabited and the largest of these was where the RAF base would be built. The natives were descendants from the crews of ships involved in the spice trade and who used the Cocos as a safe haven on their journeys to and from the Far East. They were thus a cosmopolitan, multi racial populace that had developed since the 16th Century a culture and language which reflected their mixed origins. The major European influence had been Scottish and in 1945 the King of the Cocos was a direct descendant of 'Clunis Ross', the captain of the ship's crew that had settled in the islands. Because of their isolation over the years there was virtually no disease, and the good health of the natives owed much to the temperate climate throughout the year; there were no seasons as such, everyday was like a good British summer. The economy of the islands was dependent on the copra trade - the islands being completely covered in coconut trees; the only wild life was land crabs, which scavenged in large packs and were really quite harmless.

As anticipated we disembarked without resistance and directly onto the particular island which was to be our base and airfield. The natives on Home Island across the lagoon were ordered not to leave their island, and we similarly were told that Home Island was strictly 'out of bounds'. On landing, all personnel were given a one-man tent to be shared between two! The tents were approximately seven feet long, three feet wide and two - three feet high at the apex of the pyramid shaped cross section. The squadron doctor and myself shared a tent lying lengthwise head to feet. It was some ten days before clearings among the coconut trees could be made for the erection of the more substantial Mess and accommodation tents.

The overriding priority was to get the Spitfires flying so that the island had an air defence capability. The urgency for this was increased when within three days of landing Japanese reconnaissance aircraft were seen flying over the island. The Royal Engineers had to drive a road (capable of transporting the mass of heavy equipment) through the closely packed trees. Hundreds of trees had to be felled and the ground levelled and prepared for the laying of the metal meshed surface on which the Spitfires would be operating. While this work was going on the squadron technical personnel were working flat out uncrating and assembling the aircraft. It was, as I recall, some ten days before the minimum runway length for operating the Spitfires had been reached. The approach to the runway over the trees was hazardous as was the need for the maximum rate of climb to clear the trees on take off. Only the most experienced pilots were cleared to operate until the runway length had been increased and the approach and take off paths cleared of trees. It was a credit to the pilots that during this tricky period we had only one crash, when a Spitfire's undercarriage was caught by the trees; it crashed on its back at some 160mph and it took half an hour before we could release the pilot, who was physically unscathed but somewhat mentally disturbed having anticipated that the wreck could have exploded in flames at any time. However, there was relief throughout the base that we now had an air defence capability. A Japanese attack by sea was considered a strong possibility and the Royal Navy planned to resist this with strategically positioned ships in the Indian Ocean. Within some three weeks of landing all the Spitfires had been assembled and air tested, all the pilots had commenced flying, and we were able to declare the squadron fully operational.

Shortly after arriving on the Cocos our squadron commander had been taken sick and subsequently grounded. The illness was more mental than physical and he had to be flown back to Ceylon. A brigadier of the South African Air Force was now the Commander of the Cocos. He sent for me and said I was to become the acting squadron commander until such time as a permanent appointment was made. I had mixed feelings; as a flight lieutenant I had been responsible for commanding No 9 Indian Air Force Squadron for much of the time when on operations in Burma. I thought here we go again - responsibility without the rank and permanency. I let him know my feelings while at the same time agreeing to accept the acting appointment. He was due to fly by flying boat to Ceylon for a meeting with the Commander-in-Chief. On his return he informed me that my appointment as officer commanding No 136 (F) Squadron in the rank of squadron leader had been approved by the Commander-in-Chief. He congratulated me and added wryly to make sure no Japanese bombs landed on the Cocos. I was over the moon; I had been in the RAF barely five years and had not yet reached my 23rd birthday. Now here I was - squadron leader and the commander of what was soon to be proclaimed officially the most successful fighter squadron in South East Asia. I was also gratified to discover that my appointment was popular with all sections of the squadron and the pilots in particular.

It was the following day when the excitement had died down that I thought about the implications of my new responsibilities. There was more to running a squadron than leading in the air - onerous as this was. I now had command responsibility for some 400 ground staff with their personal and family problems, and overall responsibility for the efficient workings of all sections of the squadron such as 1st and 2nd line servicing of Spitfires, a large motor transport section, clerical/admin staffs, cooks, police, medical services and so on. I must add that I think I coped OK, and I must admit getting a childish satisfaction from seeing my squadron commander's flag flying on my jeep when I was on board.

Although the squadron had started operating in mid April the Royal Engineers were having to work flat out to extend and widen the runway and provide hard standing dispersal areas in preparation for the arrival of the Liberator bomber force. Shortly after the arrival of the first Liberators I and the wing commander commanding the Liberator force had to fly to Ceylon to discuss with the Command staff the future operations, and to what extent the Spitfires, could defend the Cocos while giving protection to the Liberators on their return in daylight from their bombing missions. To do this adequately would have taken a much larger force of Spitfires and it was agreed that standing patrols over and to the south east of Cocos when the Liberators were on their return would be the best we could do. As the Liberator bombing missions got underway it became apparent that the Japanese were having to defend their South East Asia territories, and their resources were insufficient to contemplate even one or two token raids on the Cocos. But while the Allied grip tightened the Japanese continued to fight to the death in defence of their homeland and the Emperor. Kamikaze missions increased and their soldiers followed the philosophy 'kill and be killed' rather than 'kill or be killed'. So although the Allied Forces were making impressive advances they were suffering a high casualty rate. We should have been thankful that the Japanese could not afford resources to attack the Cocos; no action meant no casualties. But young pilots geared up in their Spitfires and keen to mix it with the Japanese felt somewhat cheated; this applied particularly to many of our current pilots who had not experienced operations in Burma or any other theatre of the war. As it was, we were to continue with an active air defence of the Cocos until the war had effectively ended in August, without engaging enemy aircraft or firing our guns in anger.

Flying from the Cocos in a single engined, single seat, Spitfire had its worrying aspects. Apart from the Keeling Island, a small, uninhabited tree covered island, about ten miles away from the Cocos, the nearest land was Sumatra some 800 miles away. The only navigation aid in the Spitfire was a compass so, particularly when above cloud, you had to keep a mental log of the different courses you had flown, so that you knew roughly the course you needed to return to the island. If on breaking cloud the island was not there, you had to exercise self-control and follow the discipline of flying a square search until you hopefully sighted the island. The island radar installation could help but it was not consistently reliable. If you had engine trouble there was no mother earth to force land on; you either crashed or parachuted into the sea and hoped that search Spitfires would sight your dinghy and direct a motor launch to the rescue. There was an occasion when a Mosquito aircraft took off from Australia on a reconnaissance mission, intending to land on the Cocos, having flown some 3,000 miles, when within one hour's flying from the Cocos R/T contact was lost. When the Mosquito became overdue we sent four Spitfires in different directions to see if we could contact it by R/T and give whatever help was possible, such as intercepting it and escorting it to the Cocos. As time went by it became apparent that it must have run out of fuel and come down in the sea. We now had eight Spitfires searching the sea at low level hoping to sight the three man crew dinghy, but by late afternoon we had had no sighting; one of the pilots had flown low over the Keeling Island but reported no sign of a wreck. As dusk fell it was suggested that a wreck on the island could have been hidden by the undergrowth, and that if the Mosquito had crashed and the crew survived they would by now have lit a fire, which would easily be seen from the air. By now it was getting dark and the runway lights had yet to be installed. I reckoned I had sufficient time to fly to the island and back before nightfall. I nipped off and as I approached the island I saw a fire and flying low saw the Mosquito crew waving like mad. I circled to let them know I had seen them and landed back as night fell. They were picked up by launch the following morning having suffered no injury. Their story was almost unbelievable. They had been completely lost and on descending through cloud the engines had failed through lack of fuel. To their amazement ahead of them was a small island; with undercarriage raised and flaps down they glided across onto a small beach. The Mosquito had continued on its belly and crashed into the undergrowth, coming to rest between two large trees, which had torn off both wings. Fliers need luck and they certainly had had their share that day. A few days later a second Mosquito flew in from Australia, the crew had spent two hours looking for the Cocos and on their approach had run out of fuel and crashed onto the runway. They suffered injury but recovered after hospital treatment. Shortly after this one of our pilots crashed into the sea due to engine failure. He was very badly injured but the army surgeon in the field hospital, with the help of the squadron's medical officer, performed a virtual miracle; he is still alive and little the worse for his 'multiple' injuries.

The Keeling Island had attracted a degree of publicity during the Great War. A German Cruiser, the Emden, had sunk a large number of our shipping in the Indian Ocean. It was eventually cornered and sunk by the Royal Navy off Keeling. The sea in the Cocos/Keeling area is very clear and the wreck of the Emden can be clearly seen from the air lying on its side on the bottom of the ocean.

I must now go back in time and recount what had been happening to Denise since I had last had contact with her, when she was taken to hospital following our wedding in February, - it now being June. While in hospital in Poona she had received news that her unit, Force 136, was leaving Kirkee and joining the South East Asia Command Headquarters at Kandy in Ceylon. Following four weeks in hospital and a week's leave in Aurangabad she arrived back with Force 136 in time to join them for the move to Kandy. On arrival at Kandy she was to discover that 136 Squadron was now in the Cocos Islands. I knew nothing of her move to Kandy because we were still in non-communicado. In June a Malayan dhow arrived at the Cocos Island and I received, through 'Intelligence' sources, an invitation from the captain to dine with him and his crew. I drove to the dhow's moorings in a quiet part of the Island, was picked up by a small boat and received by a Lieutenant Commander Captain who introduced me to his crew of two, - an Army Major and an RAF Flight Lieutenant. I had no idea what this was all about until they explained that they were part of Force 136. Without losing the outward appearance of a Malay dhow, the dhow had been internally reconstructed and had in particular been fitted with a very powerful engine and radio. Their operational role was to infiltrate agents into Malaya, rendezvous with them at periodic intervals, and transmit their reports back to their Headquarters in Kandy. They knew Denise and let me know that she was now fit and at Kandy; the fact that we now knew where each of us was, was comforting. That night my hosts wined and dined me well. My concern was the following morning when I awoke to find I was in the crow's nest and with a hangover. Getting down from a crow's nest was for me a hazardous operation, but to do it with a hangover and with three lunatics cheering me on was an experience I will never forget. Except when in an aeroplane, I cannot cope with heights. In wartime you make and lose friends quickly. When I eventually met with Denise it was with great sorrow she told me that the three had been killed when their dhow was sunk by a Japanese naval ship off the Malayan coast.

Throughout July the Liberators continued on the offensive with us maintaining patrols in case of Japanese intervention, which never materialised. In August the atomic bombs were dropped on Hiroshima and Nagasaki followed by the Japanese surrender. With the war thankfully coming to an end the squadron received notification that, as a squadron formed solely for wartime operations, it would shortly be disbanded. A photostat copy of the letter from the Allied Air Commander in Chief follows; it puts in a nutshell the fine record of 136 Squadron achieved against the Japanese.

When I had flown to Ceylon, to discuss the tactics we would employ to defend the Liberator force, I anticipated that I would eventually meet up with Denise for the first time since I had left her in hospital six months earlier. On arrival I discovered that she was in the air flying to Delhi to attend a conference. Her boss, who had given her away at the wedding, said she would be returning in four days. Four days later the plane returning me to the Cocos took off two hours before her plane landed at Colombo!

In mid-August I flew back to Ceylon for a week's leave. Denise met me at the airport and we took the military train to Kandy. On arriving at Kandy I had a high temperature and was taken to hospital with septicaemia. Three years before, when flying in Rangoon, I had received a small piece of metal in my back when a Japanese bullet failed to fully penetrate the armour plate. I had not regarded it more than an irritation and thought it had healed but it had flared up and turned septic.

From:- Air Marshal Sir Keith Park, K.C.B., K.B.E., M.C., D.F.C.

Headquarters
Air Command
South East Asia

DO/KRP/145.   7th August, 1945

Dear Kitley,

It is with real regret that I have had to issue instructions for the disbandment of your Squadron.

Due to reductions of our Forces demanded by Air Ministry we have had to disband several of our Squadrons, in spite of fine war records like 136 Squadron.

Since your Squadron's arrival in this Command, I note that one flight fought its way back from Rangoon in early 1942, losing all its Pilots except one, but on New Years Eve 1943 you secured an ample revenge by destroying an entire Japanese Bomber and Fighter formation.

Your Squadron also took part in the battle for the Imphal Plain contributing in no small measure to a most signal victory for our Forces.

During the Squadrons' operations in this theatre it achieved the finest "bag" of enemy aircraft by any R.A.F. Squadron in South East Asia, 100 Japanese aircraft being destroyed and 150 being probables or damaged, one third of these figures being accounted for in the first two months of 1944.

In wishing you and your Squadron personnel good luck for your future, whether it be for release or to a new appointment, I want you all to realise how much the efforts of 136 Squadron are appreciated by myself and the Air Ministry, who have had to reduce our Air Forces overseas.

S/Ldr. A.J.H. Kitley,
Officer Commanding,
No. 136 Squadron.

Yours sincerely,
Keith Park

It was my good fortune that penicillin, which had been in short supply and not available to our forces in the Far East, had now come on stream and I was one of the first to receive it. I was in hospital for my week's leave with Denise visiting me daily, on discharge I had to fly back to the Cocos.

The administrative arrangements for disbanding the squadron were now in hand, and towards the end of August we put on a flying display for the islands and finished it with an eighteen Spitfire formation flying the letters 'VJ'. We attended a number of war-ending celebration parties in the various Messes. I returned to Ceylon in September and at last enjoyed a three week leave with Denise, before we both embarked on the six week journey for the UK.

136 Squadron parade on disbandment,
Cocos Islands September 1945

Spitfire VIIIs of 136 Squadron in the Cocos Islands, Far East, September 1945. Sqn.Ldr. A.J.H. Kitley, CO. (Foundation Member of 136 in August 1941 at Kirton as Sergeant Pilot.)

*The Japs have surrendered
Cocos Islands, August 1945*

'VJ' formation following disbandment parade

CHAPTER EIGHT

LOOKING FORWARD, LOOKING BACK

On the boat journey home to the UK there was plenty of opportunity to reflect over the 5.5 years I had now been in the RAF, four of which had been serving in the Far East. I recalled the problems I had faced to join the RAF for pilot training; the resistance of my family and the misery that I must have brought to my mother; having to falsify my age; going 'absent without leave' to protest to the Air Ministry that RAF Cardington was not going to release me for pilot training. Then there was the relief when orders came through for me to commence pilot training at Torquay; the excitement of my first solo flight; getting lost over Cambridgeshire and force landing in a school playing field; under threat of being suspended; the incident with the Messerschmitt fighter; qualifying as a pilot in Canada; the distasteful passage in a Royal Navy armed merchant ship; double pneumonia in a Reykjavik hospital, my luck in being on the destroyer which did not go on the fatal 'sink the Bismarck' mission; flying a Hurricane for the first time; losing two friends in fatal crashes at the Hurricane training unit.

Joining 136 Squadron on its formation had been the start of realising what awaited us: the inevitability of having eventually to face an enemy; learning to master the Hurricane; flying it to its limits and exploiting to the full its potential as a flying machine. After being deemed fit for operations the squadron had set off by ship to join the Ark Royal; the Ark Royal was sunk; we are now off to the Caucuses to reinforce the Russians; the Japs enter the scene; by the end of the year (1941), in Rangoon after an understandably unplanned and ill prepared flight from Egypt (the Israelites under Moses had done it better); fighting a Japanese Air Force which outnumbered us by some fifteen to one; retreating north and eventually being shot out of the sky, flying sub standard Hurricanes, at Akyab; licking our wounds in Calcutta; building up squadron strength; operating from a road in the middle of Calcutta; returning to Chittagong by the end of 1942; flying and fighting hard in the

Arakan in support of the Army; attacking Japanese ground forces; sorties across the formidable Chin Hills into central and southern Burma attacking lines of communication; fighting and warding off attacks by the Japanese Air Force.

By May 1943 I had completed a full operational tour of 200 hours and posted to Risalpur for a 'rest'. The 'rest' may have been from operational flying, but converting newly qualified pilots to operational flying in Hurricanes had been no picnic. During my six months at Risalpur I had experienced a mixture of emotions: remorse at the high number of fatal accidents our trainees suffered; apprehension with the Japanese threat being replaced by the threat of being flown into by an over enthusiastic trainee; pleasure in having living conditions which, regardless of the excessive heat, were far removed from the monsoons, mud huts and goat stew; self pity while suffering a miscellany of sickness involving heat exhaustion, jaundice, pneumonia (again!) dysentery and stomach ulcers.

The beginning of 1944 had seen me promoted and posted as flight commander to No 9 IAF Squadron, which was to form at Bhopal in central India. The next seven months had been pretty hectic: moving to the forward, operational area; having to continue training the pilots while flying with them on operational sorties; suffering, and coping with, a high casualty rate; appalling monsoon weather; attempting to manage the clash of cultural, religious and political loyalties endemic within the Indians and which could undermine team cohesiveness. The pressures were such that having had to fly a record 45 operational hours in May, June had seen me in hospital for four weeks with dysentery and pleurisy.

Poona had been a bit of a doddle; training yes, but as a flight commander I had sufficient instructors to take it easy. Most of my activities had centred on wooing and marrying Denise. Next unbelievably, came the posting back to 136 Squadron as flight commander, followed by promotion to squadron leader and command of the squadron, now equipped with Spitfires. The anticlimax was that Far East Command Headquarters, having ordered the development of a large bomber base on the Cocos Islands to be defended by 136 Squadron, the Japanese started to crumble and the two atom bombs ensured that our, and the American forces were not to suffer the very high casualties that had been anticipated if we had had to win the war with conventional weapons.

What effect had these five years of experiences had on me? Had I changed and if so, how had I changed? Certainly, the immature eighteen year old, who had been reduced to tears when verbally abused that night in a tent in Cardington, was now at twenty three years of age a reasonably confident character who could give as good, if not more, than he got. I now had an authority which had developed hand in hand with the increasing responsibilities I had been progressively given. In the early days in Burma those responsibilities had been mainly those of a leader in the air. As a flight commander these responsibilities increased, to embrace the management of the technical servicing facilities and the personnel representing the wide range of specialists trades needed to maintain aircraft serviceability and readiness. It was then that I became aware of the importance of inter dependency; that all members of a squadron, air and ground personnel, officers, SNCOs and airmen had vital jobs to do and that the product of all those jobs had to come together to ensure optimum squadron effectiveness. It's no good having an ace pilot in a super fighter aircraft if on take off the undercarriage does not retract or when the firing button is pressed the guns jam. Thus the principle of inter dependence was one that, on looking back, I realised had been applied by Squadron Leader Elsdon when he formed the squadron in 1941; its strength was its simplicity and the only way to command or manage if in the end you want the 'whole' to be greater than the sum of its individual parts. During a war life and death and advancement is somewhat of a lottery. You have to be competent but promotion opportunities and increased responsibilities come, in the main, from filling dead men's shoes and being in the right place at the right time. I had progressed from sergeant to the rank of squadron leader in four years, but I was realistic enough to know that opportunity and luck had played a part in that success. But I have to admit that I was proud of my achievement in being given command of 136 Squadron, which was now being commended by the powers that be for its successful record in operations against the Japanese.

The responsibilities of fighter pilots and their leaders are interwoven throughout this narrative and need no embellishment. But in a nutshell the responsibilities of the commanding officer of a mobile fighter squadron were formidable. 136 Squadron had become such a mobile squadron with some 400 ground crew, 35 pilots, 22 Spitfires and a wide range of vehicles and equipment needed to resource a squadron operating independently of the support of its home base. The commanding officer also had the sole responsibility for the air defence of, in this case, the Cocos Islands and the large bomber force operating there. On looking back I wonder how, at the age of twenty three years, I was able to shoulder those responsibilities. But my circumstances were not unique; many fighter squadron commanders under the age of thirty years, had similar responsibilities. This leads me to reflect on our youth of today; they are regarded by many as badly behaved, inconsiderate and selfish, and many deserve such criticism. But does this not stem from a lack of challenge, a lack of opportunity to take responsibility? If so, we need government and industry, to assist development of a socio economic structure that provides opportunity for youth to develop its potential through the exercise of responsibility. What a waste of potential talent if it can only be released in a war situation.

At the beginning of the war, tactical air warfare had seen the 'fighter' as essentially operating in an air-to-air combat role. Following our success in the Battle of Britain, this was understandably how the British public saw a 'fighter's' role; in this case protecting Britain by shooting down or repelling enemy aircraft. However, as the war progressed, the need for the 'fighter' to adapt and take on a multi-purpose role became apparent; this was particularly so in the Far East. The Hurricane proved to be particularly adaptable to undertake the wider role. In air-to-ground operations, increasing the armament from eight to twelve Browning machine guns with a spread harmonisation, made it very effective when attacking enemy troops and vehicles. The wing strength of the Hurricane allowed for the mounting of jettisonable long-range tanks; this increased the operating range and the time spent in the air and thus widened the area of operations. Towards the end of 1943, when Spitfires became available to concentrate more on the air-to-air role, the Hurricane was adapted further to carry bombs and rockets. In the Middle East some Hurricanes were able to be modified to carry two heavy anti-aircraft 40 mm Bofors guns; very effective fire power when attacking enemy tanks. Towards the end of the war some of these diverse roles were taken over by purpose built fighters such as Typhoons. But these aircraft were allocated to the European theatre and not made available to the Far East.

The contribution made by the Hurricane to the air war in the Far East demonstrates what a fine war-horse it was, - fast, highly manoeuvrable and robust. It could take punishment while giving protection to the pilot. For example: the crash at Bahrain when my injury was limited to no more than superficial cuts on the hand; when, on returning from a raid on Moulmein airfield, I hit the sea but still managed to make Rangoon in spite of a badly damaged propeller; in the early days at Rangoon, treating with contempt the bullets of the then Japanese fighters that could not penetrate effectively the armour plate behind the pilot's back; keeping flying with minimum servicing and with sub-standard locally manufactured 'spares'; finally keeping on flying in spite of the Hurricane doctors telling it that it was 'unfit for operations'. But praise for the Hurricane being able to adapt to a multi-purpose role, must go hand in hand with that for the pilots and ground crews; they had to 'train on the job' to cope with the changing demands and with a 'suck it and see' technique which did not help the accident statistics.

Apart from the Japanese, our main threat had been the weather and climatic conditions. The monsoons could present a flying hazard which would have challenged the most experienced pilots; for pilots of limited experience the conditions could at times be impossible. But, and understandably, flying had to continue in spite of such weather. The turbulence and up currents in a cumulo nimbus cloud towering up to 45,000 feet, could at worst break up an aeroplane or at best carry it up and disgorge it out of control at heights of up to 40,000 feet. Chapter 4 (The Red Road Runway) refers to the tragic consequences of a squadron of Spitfires which entered such a cloud. All clouds forming over mountain ranges such as the Chin Hills had a high degree of turbulence; this could cause the aeroplane's instruments to behave erratically and the pilot to have difficulty in maintaining control. Having to operate from temporary jungle airstrips which were narrow, of limited length and surrounded by jungle, involved a high accident rate. Approaching the airstrips in strong wind gusts and intense monsoon rain which restricted visibility was a challenge in itself, and if you landed without mishap you then faced the hazard of a water logged and uneven runway. Apart from unreliable radio communication the Hurricane had two navigation aids, - compass and a pilot's grey matter. After flying for some time over cloud cover, these were the two aids the pilot relied on to ensure that when descending through cloud, the Hurricane did not crash into high ground. The majority of reinforcement pilots sent out to us were, as we had been, straight from training and had to gain their flying experience in these difficult conditions. To be realistic, accidents had to be anticipated when flying safety had to have a lower priority than the needs of war. Finally, our living conditions, particularly in Burma, had given rise to much petty but debilitating sickness, which adversely affected the abilities of both air and ground crews to perform at maximum effectiveness. Flying or servicing aircraft in very hot temperatures and high humidity, while suffering from dhobi itch, prickly heat, and various other skin infections, and while suffering the after effects of sandfly, malaria or other fevers, is not conducive to high performance.

In spite of the battering we had taken in 1942/43, there had been an understanding and albeit reluctant acceptance that winning the war in Europe and the Middle East had to be the number one priority. Success or even failure in the Far East would have been of little consequence if Germany had overrun Britain, Europe and the Middle East. As a consequence reinforcements and better equipment were slow in coming. What did rankle was that the British forces had not been well served with senior commanders at General and Air Marshal level; they tended to be those who had not come up to scratch in their Commands at crucial stages of the war in Europe and the Middle East. They were officers who had served their country well in the Great War and inter war years, but had been shown to lack initiative, flexibility of mind and appreciation of the changing nature of modern warfare.

They were inclined to be aloof and to protect themselves behind somewhat sycophantic officers such as ADCs and personal staff officers. This, coupled with an over bureautic and extended chain of command between them and their fighting units, meant that they were seen by their airmen and soldiers as faceless commanders, who were indifferent to their difficulties and problems. But as the war in Europe and the Middle East started going in our favour so, along with reinforcements and equipment, we had begun to get the younger, active war experienced senior commanders. One such had been a new 'Air Commander-in-Chief', Air Marshall Sir Keith Park. He had commanded the famous No. 11 Group in the Battle of Britain. As ACinC he brought a breath of fresh air and a sense of urgency to his command. He impressed all by flying and visiting many of his units in his own Hurricane. He earned the respect of both his air and ground crews, talked their language and had that indefinable trait - charisma. He concerned himself with the general inadequate living conditions of all ranks, by arranging for a better provision of basic needs! For example, razor-blades, soap, beer and where possible food and accommodation. Lord Mountbatten and General Slim were further examples of the type of commanders we could have done with in the 43/44 years. As it was, the morale throughout the Royal Air Force in the Far East improved with the knowledge that we now had ACinC who was competent, 'with it' and had a high regard for those who served under him.

The repetitive, boring and lazy routine of the ship afforded an opportunity and appropriate atmosphere to think about the many close friends I had made and those who had been killed. Of the twenty eight pilots of No 136 Squadron who had left England in November 1941, twenty one had been killed along with those who had progressively joined the squadron as replacements. There had also been the fatalities of similar scale in the Indian Air Force squadron during the six month period I had flown with them in Burma. They were all pilots with whom I had lived and flown and I found it difficult to understand how we had been able to cope with the effects of such deaths; how we were able to put the grief behind us and maintain the operational flying momentum. There was now a peaceful opportunity to grieve, but I found that passage of time had made it difficult to conjure up grief. I was however, able to reflect and consider what brave and resolute pilots and friends they had been. Denise had also lost friends and colleagues working with the 'Special' Forces in France and the Far East; she also had difficulty unbottling the grief. We entered Southampton on the morning of 11th November 1945 while the Armistice Service was being held. For both of us, that Service and particularly the two minutes silence said it all. But reference to this nostalgic sadness does not create the right mood on which to finish this book. I had spent four years contributing to the defeat of Japan. I had made and still had many wartime comrades. Not only had I survived but I had had the unique good fortune to meet and marry Denise. Our marriage was to last 46 years until her death. We had three cracking good children, - one son and two daughters. By the turn of the century all three were to each celebrate their Silver Weddings and had presented us with seven grandchildren; what more could anyone want?

Many people have referred to what they assume must have been a period approaching four years of carnage and misery. Did I enjoy the war? Do I regret the experience? Just think! - at eighteen years of age and at a time when a bicycle was the fastest machine I, and most of my peers had ridden, I had been given aeroplanes such as the Hurricane and Spitfire to fly and fight in. In spite of setbacks, losses of life, I have only one answer to the question 'Did I enjoy it?' - you bet I did!

MAPS

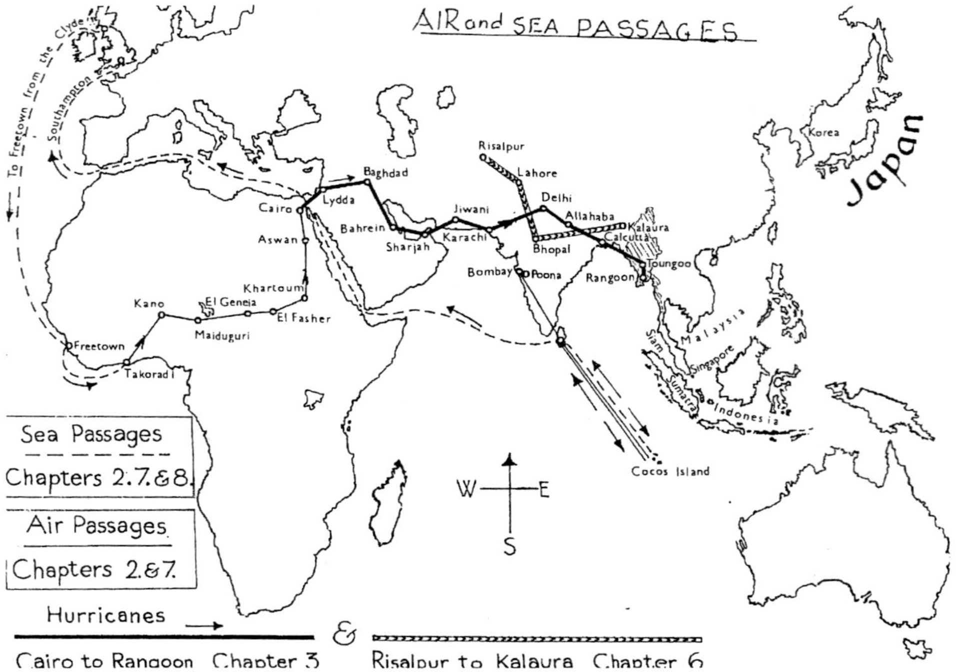
AIR and SEA PASSAGES
To Freetown from the Clyde
Southampton
Japan
Korea
Risalpur
Lahore
Baghdad
Lydda
Cairo
Delhi
Jiwani
Allahaba
Kalaura
Calcutta
Bahrein
Sharjah
Karachi
Bhopal
Aswan
Bombay
Poona
Toungoo
Rangoon
Khartoum
Kano
El Geneia
El Fasher
Maiduguri
Freetown
Takoradi
Malaysia
Siam
Singapore
Sumatra
Indonesia
Cocos Island
W
E
S
Sea Passages
Chapters 2.7.&8.
Air Passages
Chapters 2.&7.
Hurricanes
Cairo to Rangoon Chapter 3
&
Risalpur to Kalaura Chapter 6

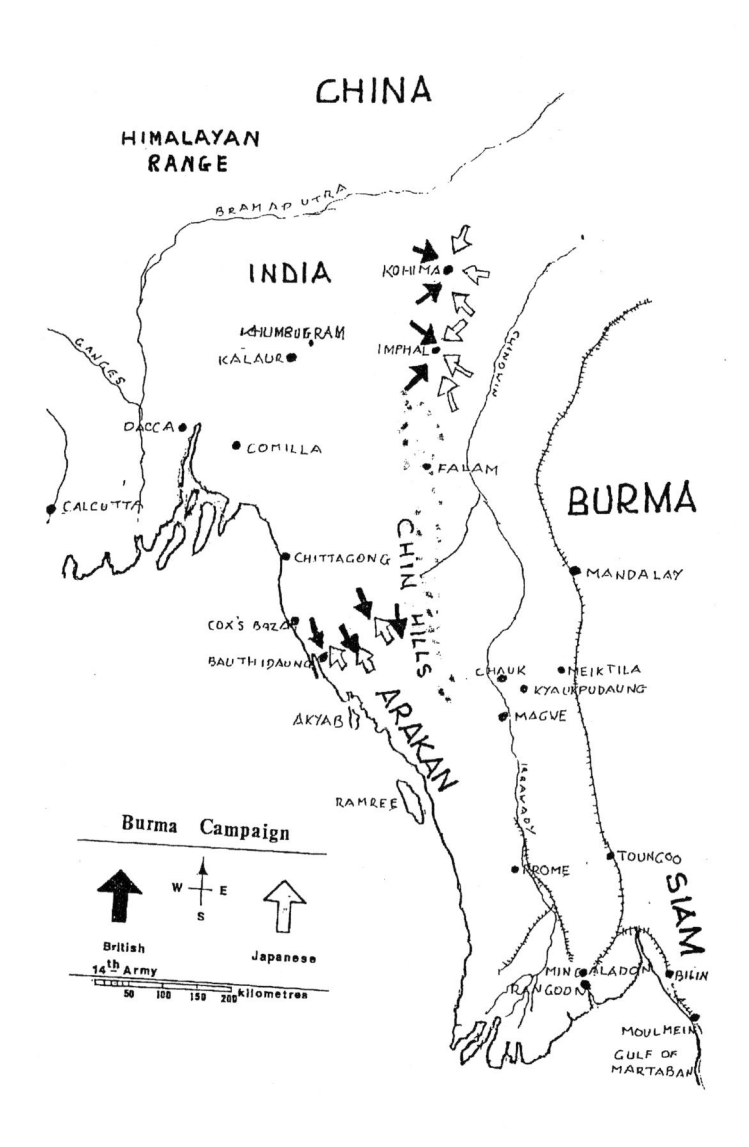